Gingerbread

TIMELESS RECIPES FOR CAKES, COOKIES, DESSERTS, ICE CREAM, AND CANDY

By Jennifer Lindner McGlinn

Photographs by Béatrice Peltre

CHRONICLE BOOKS
SAN FRANCISCO

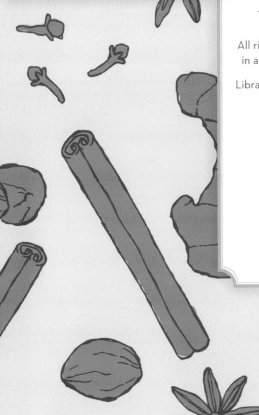

→ To my family, who so lovingly support my dreams and endeavors. ←
To Antonia Allegra and Don and Joan Fry, who are the best friends and mentors a writer could ever hope to have.

Text copyright © 2009 by Jennifer Lindner McGlinn
Photographs copyright © 2009 by Béatrice Peltre

All rights reserved. No part of this book may be reproduced
in any form without written permission from the publisher.

Library of Congress Cataloging-in-Publication Data available.

ISBN: 978-0-8118-6191-5

Manufactured in China

Designed by Catherine Grishaver

10 9 8 7 6 5 4 3 2 1

Chronicle Books LLC
680 Second Street
San Francisco, California 94107

www.chroniclebooks.com

Introduction

I have loved gingerbread for as long as I can remember. It all started with a recipe I found in one of my grandmother's cookbooks. She had a wonderful array of recipe books, pamphlets, and magazines, some dating from the 1930s. I always had a particular fondness, though, for her 1950 edition of *Betty Crocker's New Picture Cook Book*. I loved this binder-like collection with its old-fashioned recipes, fluorescent-colored photographs, and illustrations of pretty women wearing big skirts and high heels as they cooked. When my grandmother gave me her beloved *Betty Crocker*, I decided it was time I tried the recipe for Favorite Gingerbread that had intrigued me for years.

The ingredients were basic and the method was easy to follow. A handheld mixer, square baking pan, some measuring cups and spoons, and a spatula were the only tools I needed to get the job done. The results exceeded my expectations. As the cake baked, it filled the kitchen with enticing, soul-satisfying aromas. Once I retrieved the mahogany-colored gingerbread from the oven, things got even better. My sisters and I cut squares of the warm cake and mounded billowy clouds of soft whipped cream on top. Moist, spicy, and sweet with molasses, the gingerbread took well to the cream, which promptly began melting into the warm crumbs. The dessert was soothing and satisfying in the way that only simple, old-fashioned dishes can be. It's no wonder that this cake has been one of my favorite comfort foods ever since.

What comes to mind when *you* think of gingerbread? Perhaps you, too, envision gingerbread cake, dark with molasses and warm with spices. Then again, maybe crispy, crinkle-topped gingersnaps come to mind. Or perhaps you recall baking and decorating cutout gingerbread girls and boys at Christmas. And who could forget gingerbread houses? Whether decorated with gumdrops, pretzels, and candy canes, or with fancy sugar work and marzipan, these whimsical structures take homemade gingerbread to an entirely new level of artistry and skill.

Then there are the gingerbreads that hail from other parts of the world. Orange-scented, honey-sweetened cookies called *Lebkuchen* date back to fourteenth-century Germany. *Pain d'épices*, from the Burgundian region of France, is a sweet spice bread flavored with honey, citrus, and aniseed. Siena, Italy, boasts *panforte*, a spicy fruit-and-nut confection. And fruitcake, the traditional British Christmas cake, is dense with dried fruit, fragrant with spices, and cloaked in marzipan and rolled fondant. Indeed, there are many more examples to be had, but you get the idea. Gingerbread encompasses a wide variety of sweet, spicy treats, many of which date back centuries.

The history of gingerbread is a long and colorful one, indeed. Native to Indo-Malaysia, ginger has been cultivated in subtropical Asia for more than 3,000 years. The Greeks and Romans, as well as the Chinese and Arabs, relished this spice, using it to flavor many sweet and savory dishes, including honeyed spice breads and cakes. By the Middle Ages, ginger was on the move. The Crusaders returned to Europe from the Middle East with ginger among their wide array of newfound foodstuffs and exotic spices. As ginger gained popularity in European kitchens, it continued to spread across the globe, as well. The Portuguese began growing a unique variety of ginger in Africa, and by the sixteenth century, the Spanish were cultivating what became high-quality Jamaican ginger in the West Indies.

Some of the early European gingerbreads probably resembled the Chinese spice breads from centuries earlier. Honey-sweetened, anise-scented *pain d'épices* gained great favor in France as early as 1393. At the same time, honey-based *Lebkuchen* was developing a following in Nuremberg, Germany, with the first recorded *Lebkuchen* bakers dating to 1395. Gingerbread guilds eventually formed in Reims and Nuremberg (in 1571 and 1643, respectively), revealing the authority and places of honor these bakers held in their communities.

Other medieval gingerbreads took quite different forms. In Britain, sugar- or honey-sweetened gingerbread was usually bound with bread crumbs instead of flour. Heavily spiced and often flavored with the likes of claret wine, vinegar, rosewater, and ground almonds, the batters were either beaten into stiff pastes or cooked until thickened. They were then colored or left plain, formed into shapes or pressed into decorative wooden or ceramic molds, and left to dry.

By the late seventeenth century, this medieval-style gingerbread fell out of favor, and softer baked gingerbreads sweetened with molasses and treacle began to emerge. Rolled and shaped spice cakes (cookies, really) frequently appeared in eighteenth-century British cookery books and became popular in America, as well. Eventually, though, Americans developed a fondness for even more tender gingerbread cakes. By the late 1700s, home cooks had been using pearl ash (potassium bicarbonate) for years to lighten baked goods rich with eggs, butter, cream, and sugar. However, it wasn't until American-born Amelia Simmons published her *American Cookery* in 1796 that this leavener appeared in print, along with no less than five of her gingerbread recipes. Many writers eventually followed Simmons's lead. As authors such as Eliza Leslie, Lydia Maria Child, and Fannie Merritt Farmer wrote about American cooking and baking, they continued to compile recipes for all sorts of gingerbread cakes and cookies. Happily, the trend has continued.

If spicy, molasses-rich cake enticed me to fall for gingerbread as a child, many other gingery treats have further seduced me as an adult. From cakes and cookies to desserts and breakfast treats to confections and ice creams to fanciful spiced structures, gingerbread takes many delicious forms. Although all the recipes in this book call for ginger in some form (powdered, crystallized, or fresh), you will find that the ancillary ingredients are flavorfully varied. Molasses, brown sugar, and spices, such as cinnamon, cloves, nutmeg, and allspice, appear frequently, but not always. You will find gingerbreads sweetened with honey and golden syrup; spiced with aniseed, cardamom, coriander, Chinese five-spice powder, and mustard powder; flavored with citrus, chocolate, and rum; and textured with oat bran and almond and rice flours. Some are moist, soft, and as dark as ebony, while others are crisp, firm, and golden blond.

Most of us have come to think of gingerbread as an exclusively fall and winter dessert, and understandably so. Who wouldn't want to cuddle up by the fire with a batch of soft molasses cookies or a warm square of fragrant gingerbread cake? With its many enticing varieties, however, gingerbread certainly deserves to be celebrated year-round. Whether you like your gingerbread vibrant with spices or delicately perfumed, warm right out of the oven or firm and chilled from the freezer, there are plenty of ways to enjoy it no matter the season.

Every time I make gingerbread, I think of my grandmother and the book that inspired me to bake my first spicy cake. Maybe the best thing about gingerbread is that with its old-fashioned appeal, it satisfies us in ways that only home-style, comforting food can. I hope the flavors and aromas of these treats will remind you, too, of happy times, or inspire you to create new memories filled with warm, gingery goodness.

Equipment

The equipment I find helpful for making gingerbread will serve you well in all of your baking endeavors. Here are some pieces I like best.

STAND MIXER

With only a few exceptions, all of my recipes call for using a stand mixer—one that comes with a stainless-steel bowl and that can be fitted with paddle and whisk attachments. You can certainly use a handheld mixer if you prefer, but I often find it more cumbersome and less efficient than the stand type. I like having the freedom to walk away from whipping egg whites or a beating batter for a minute or two to attend to another task while letting the machine do the work.

BAKING PANS

Having a variety of pans at the ready is a good idea if you bake a fair number of cakes and bar cookies. With a few round cake pans, square baking pans, tube pans, springform pans, and loaf pans, you can bake practically anything. I sometimes like to use the nonstick versions of these vessels, but most of the time, I like heavy-gauge, aluminum-coated steel pans. Try not to use pans with dark finishes, as I find they result in cakes that brown too quickly in the oven.

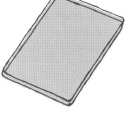

BAKING SHEETS

Good-quality baking sheets are essential to successful cookies of all kinds. I suggest purchasing professional-weight baking sheets. Unlike lighter-weight supermarket types, which tend to warp after a while, these heavy-gauge baking sheets will remain flat even after years of use. I prefer aluminum-coated steel sheets to the darker types, as they produce lighter-colored cookies. Having a variety of sizes at the ready is a good idea, but I particularly like the large 17¼-by-11½-by-1-inch baking sheets (also called half-sheet pans) or 15½-by-10½-by-1-inch baking sheets the best.

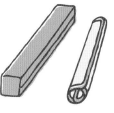

BAKING SHEET LINERS

To make baking and cleanup as easy as possible, I like to line my baking sheets with parchment paper or silicone-coated liners. I find that I can reuse a sheet of parchment paper several times, and silicone liners require only a simple wipe-down or quick wash in the sink after each use.

WIRE RACKS

It's helpful to have several wire racks on hand for cooling cookies and cakes. They are also useful for glazing large or small items, allowing the excess glaze to drip neatly off of and away from the bases.

Ingredients

Great gingerbread requires only a handful of easy-to-find, easy-to-store ingredients. Here is a basic list of what you will need to bake a variety of successful, spicy treats.

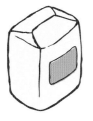

FLOUR

I use all-purpose flour in just about all of my gingerbreads. Sometimes, especially in a number of gingerbread cakes, I do prefer, and call for, cake flour. Because of its high starch and low gluten content, this fine-textured flour makes for light and tender cakes. If you need to substitute all-purpose flour in a pinch, follow this method: For every 1 cup of cake flour, use 1 cup minus 2 tablespoons of all-purpose flour.

ALMOND FLOUR

Only a few of my recipes call for almond flour, but I include it here because it really adds a lovely, mildly nutty flavor and soft texture to gingerbread. It is sold in most supermarkets (usually in the organic or health-food section) as almond flour or almond meal. The ingredient list on the package should contain nothing but finely ground almonds. If you don't have almond flour, just grind up some almonds to as fine a powder as you can in a food processor.

SUGAR

I use a variety of sugars in my gingerbread recipes. Granulated sugar appears frequently, as does brown sugar. Molasses gives light and dark brown sugars their characteristic caramel-like flavors, and both impart warmth and richness to gingerbread. To measure brown sugar, pack it into measuring cups, pressing lightly with your fingers.

MOLASSES

Molasses is produced during the refining process of sugarcane. Sugarcane juice is boiled and reduced to a syrupy mixture, some of which crystallizes and is removed, and some of which remains in a dark liquid form. This is molasses. It is then boiled two more times. Each time, as more sugar is removed, the molasses becomes darker and increasingly bitter.

The first boiling produces light or mild molasses. It is dark chestnut in color and, as its name implies, has a mild, sweet flavor. The second boiling produces dark molasses. It is dark mahogany in color, thick, and has a more intense flavor. The third and last boiling produces blackstrap molasses. It is so dark as to appear almost black and has a very bitter flavor.

In the past, sulfur dioxide has been added to molasses to produce a clearer product, but it was found to contribute an off-putting chemical taste. Today, most molasses is left unsulfured. Readily available in supermarkets, unsulfured molasses has a purer sugarcane flavor. There are many brands from which to choose, each with a slightly different character and flavor. Have fun trying them and see which you like best.

Most of the recipes in this book call simply for molasses without specifying light or dark. (I don't call for any blackstrap.) For the most part, I encourage you to use what you like. If you prefer a mild flavor in your baking, use the light. If you want more of an intense molasses experience, use the dark. You could even mix a little of each. The only time I specify using dark molasses is when I want to give the recipe a vibrant punch without adding too much liquid or sugar to the dough or batter. Again, use your own discretion. If you still prefer the light variety, go ahead and add it instead.

SPICES

There are a number of spices you will want to keep on hand when baking gingerbread. In some cases, it is fine to purchase them already ground. Good-quality cinnamon, allspice, mace, and cloves are available already ground. Aniseed is also available already ground, or, if you prefer, grind up whole star anise instead. As for nutmeg, it might sound trendy, but I do think it's best freshly grated. Whole nutmeg is readily available these days in gourmet stores and some supermarkets. Use a nutmeg grater if you wish, or simply use a Microplane rasp or fine-toothed grater. I like to store my whole and ground spices in jars and keep them in the refrigerator or freezer to prevent them from spoiling quickly. Stored in this way, they should keep fresh for at least several months.

GINGER

Ginger, of course, holds a special place among the other spices, given its significance to the character and flavor of gingerbread. I use ginger in several forms throughout the book: ground, crystallized (candied), and fresh. Each contributes a particular personality to gingerbread. Ground ginger is robust and peppery. Crystallized ginger is fresh ginger that has been cooked in sugar syrup and coated with sugar. It can be mild or quite hot and adds a sweet-pungent flavor to cookies and cakes. When roughly chopped, it lends a pleasantly chewy, sugary texture to these items as well. Fresh ginger can be grated into doughs and batters, but I prefer to infuse it into liquids. It contributes a soft spiciness when steeped in the milk or cream component of a recipe and a sharper, hotter flavor when infused into sugary glazes and syrups. Whether you purchase young or spring (thin-skinned) ginger or mature (thick-skinned) ginger, choose pieces that are firm and smooth. Ginger that is wrinkled will inevitably be dry and tough. Wrapped well in plastic wrap or sealed in a zip-top bag, fresh ginger will keep fresh in the refrigerator for up to 3 weeks.

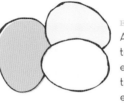

EGGS

All of my recipes call for large, room-temperature eggs. Not only will cold eggs fail to contribute as much volume to a cake batter as room-temperature eggs, but they also are more difficult to incorporate into a fluffy mixture of butter and sugar, often causing it to appear curdled. Egg whites should also be warmed to room temperature. They will whip up into fluffier, fuller meringues than whites that are firm and cold right from the refrigerator. To warm chilled eggs quickly and easily, immerse them in a bowl of warm water for about 10 minutes before using them.

BUTTER

As stated in the recipes, always use unsalted butter, as it allows you to control the saltiness of a dish yourself.

My love for gingerbread began with cake—nothing fancy, just a square of moist chestnut-colored goodness, still warm from the oven and fragrant with molasses and spices, best served with a dollop of delicately sweetened, softly whipped cream. I ate slowly, waiting for the cool cream to relinquish its fluffiness to the warm gingerbread, and and I was always left with a comforting plate of saucy, sweet crumbs.

CHAPTER ONE: Cakes

Plain, straightforward gingerbread is still my favorite, but over the years, I have found other wonderful versions, too. Some are simple and modest, while others are a bit more complex and elegant. From a nineteenth-century-inspired gingerbread brightened with lemon to a gingerbread topped with walnuts and doused with rum to a layered gingerbread filled with crunchy meringue and glossy praline buttercream, I have indeed discovered many tempting gingerbread cakes. All represent gingerbread's delicious versatility, and remind me why I fell in love with that seductive square of spicy comfort so long ago.

When I was a young girl, my paternal grandmother, Hedwig Zalewski Lindner, gave me her 1950 edition of *Betty Crocker's New Picture Cook Book*. Among the binder-bound pages covered with my grandmother's handwritten notes and various specks of salad dressing and butter, I discovered a recipe for Favorite Gingerbread. It was the first gingerbread I prepared myself, and for years it became my staple recipe. Eventually, though, I began tinkering with it to make it my own. Substituting butter for shortening, adding a bit more spice here and there, and playing with a variety of cake pans and baking times, I soon developed my own favorite gingerbread, which I now share with you. To be honest, I really don't know whether my grandmother ever made this gingerbread cake. It doesn't really matter, though. To me, it is enough that this recipe originates from a book she used so often. Preparing it, like leafing through her copy of *Betty Crocker*, reminds me of her and the many delicious, comforting dishes she prepared. This cake comes together easily and can be baked in a variety of festive pans. Bake it in an 8-cup Bundt pan, as suggested here, in a 9-inch square pan, or fill muffin tins or mini-Bundt pans about two-thirds full with batter. As you play with different shapes and sizes, just be sure to keep watch and adjust the baking times, allowing fewer minutes for smaller items.

Grandmom Lindner's Favorite Gingerbread Cake

MAKES ONE 8-CUP BUNDT CAKE

2½ cups cake flour

1 teaspoon baking soda

½ teaspoon salt

1½ teaspoons ground ginger

1 teaspoon ground cinnamon

¼ teaspoon ground allspice

¼ teaspoon ground cloves

½ cup (1 stick) unsalted butter at room temperature

¼ cup packed dark brown sugar

1 cup molasses

1 teaspoon vanilla extract

1 large egg

1 cup hot water

Whipped Cream (page 132) for serving (optional)

Position a rack in the middle of the oven and preheat the oven to 350ºF. Butter and flour an 8-cup Bundt pan.

Whisk together the cake flour, baking soda, salt, ginger, cinnamon, allspice, and cloves in a large bowl.

Put the butter in the bowl of an electric mixer fitted with the paddle attachment and beat on medium-high speed until smooth. Add the brown sugar and beat until light and fluffy. Pour in the molasses and beat until smooth. Add the vanilla extract, drop in the egg, and mix until incorporated, stopping at least once to scrape the sides of the bowl. Reduce the mixing speed to medium-low and alternately incorporate the flour mixture and hot water, beginning and ending with the flour mixture and stopping once or twice to scrape the sides of the bowl.

Pour the batter into the prepared pan and bake for about 45 minutes, or until a wooden skewer inserted near the center comes out clean. Set the gingerbread on a wire rack to cool in the pan for about 15 minutes before turning out to cool for about 10 minutes more.

Serve the cake warm or at room temperature, cut into wedges, and with dollops of the Whipped Cream, if desired.

I wanted to create a cake that not only celebrated the sweet-and-spicy qualities of old-fashioned gingerbread, but one that also featured the fine grain and density of traditional buttery pound cake. Success came rather slowly. Despite its popularity and ubiquity, consistently moist, close-grained pound cake can be challenging to bake. Altering tried-and-true formulas, such as by incorporating dark brown sugar and molasses, makes the task even trickier. I do believe I found success with this version, however. Tender, rich, and buttery, it is also warm with spices and comfortingly sweet with molasses. This pound cake is so dense and satisfying that it pairs as well with a cold glass of milk at snack time as it does with a demitasse of espresso for dessert.

Gingerbread Pound Cake

MAKES ONE 9-BY-5-BY-3-INCH LOAF CAKE

2 cups cake flour
1 teaspoon baking powder
$3/4$ teaspoon salt
$2^1/2$ teaspoons ground ginger
2 teaspoons ground cinnamon
1 teaspoon ground cloves
$1/2$ teaspoon freshly grated nutmeg

1 cup (2 sticks) unsalted butter at room temperature
$3/4$ cup granulated sugar
$1/2$ cup packed dark brown sugar
$1/2$ cup molasses
$1^1/2$ teaspoons vanilla extract
5 large eggs

Position a rack in the middle of the oven and preheat the oven to 325ºF. Butter and flour a 9-by-5-by-3-inch loaf pan.

Whisk together the cake flour, baking powder, salt, ginger, cinnamon, cloves, and nutmeg in a medium bowl.

Put the butter in the bowl of an electric mixer fitted with the paddle attachment and beat on medium-high speed until smooth. Add the granulated and brown sugars and beat until light and fluffy. Pour in the molasses and beat until smooth. Add the vanilla extract and drop in the eggs, one at time, beating for about 2 minutes and stopping at least once to scrape the sides of the bowl. Reduce the mixing speed to medium-low and gradually add the flour mixture, beating just until incorporated.

Pour the batter into the prepared pan and bake for about 1 hour and 15 minutes, or until the cake is dark chestnut brown in color, the top is cracked, and a wooden skewer inserted in the center comes out clean. Set the cake on a wire rack to cool in the pan for about 15 minutes before turning out to cool completely.

Serve the pound cake cut into $1/4$- to $1/2$-inch-thick slices.

Combining the sweet, squashy flavors of pumpkin and the spicy, molasses-rich sweetness of gingerbread, this cake represents the best of fall comfort food. More gingerbready than pumpkiny, the squash plays a supportive role in this cake. It adds moistness and sweetness to the gingerbread, as well as a delicate pumpkin flavor that supports and enhances the cake's spicy richness. As it bakes, the gingerbread acquires a deep chestnut-colored patina and tender, moist crumb. Dark molasses lends a rich caramel flavor to the gingerbread, but if you wish to make a lighter, less intense version, simply use mild molasses instead. Although it is tempting to serve the cake warm, try to wait until it has cooled. This will prevent the sliced wedges from breaking apart and enable you to appreciate their soft texture even more.

Pumpkin-Gingerbread Cake

MAKES ONE 10-INCH CAKE

3 cups all-purpose flour
2 teaspoons baking powder
2 teaspoons baking soda
1 teaspoon salt
1 tablespoon ground ginger
1 1/2 teaspoons ground cinnamon
1/2 teaspoon freshly grated nutmeg
1/2 teaspoon ground cloves
1 cup (2 sticks) unsalted butter at room temperature

1 cup granulated sugar
1/2 cup packed light brown sugar
1/2 cup dark molasses
4 large eggs
2 teaspoons vanilla extract
2 1/4 cups pumpkin purée
2 tablespoons finely chopped crystallized ginger

Vanilla Ice Cream (page 134) for serving (optional)

Position a rack in the middle of the oven and preheat the oven to 350ºF. Butter and flour a 10-inch tube pan.

Whisk together the flour, baking powder, baking soda, salt, ginger, cinnamon, nutmeg, and cloves in a large bowl.

Put the butter in the bowl of an electric mixer fitted with the paddle attachment and beat on medium-high speed until smooth. Add the granulated and brown sugars and beat until light and fluffy. Pour in the molasses and beat until smooth. Drop in the eggs, one at time, and beat for about 2 minutes, stopping at least once to scrape the sides of the bowl. Add the vanilla extract, pumpkin purée, and crystallized ginger, mixing until combined. Reduce the mixing speed to medium-low and gradually add the flour mixture, beating just until incorporated.

Pour the batter into the prepared pan and bake for about 1 hour, or until the cake is dark chestnut brown in color, the top is cracked, and a wooden skewer inserted near the center comes out clean. Set the cake on a wire rack to cool in the pan for about 15 minutes before turning out to cool completely.

Serve the cake cut into wedges and with the Vanilla Ice Cream, if desired.

There is something so approachable and delightfully old-fashioned about simply frosted layer cakes. This apple-enriched gingerbread version is no exception. Apple butter not only lends moistness to the cake, but its caramelized, slightly tart flavor also complements the warm spiciness of the gingerbread. Buttery and packed with brown sugar, the butterscotch-flavored, slightly (and delightfully) grainy frosting marries deliciously with these tender layers and is easy to apply as well. No professional cake turntable or special pastry palette knife is required here. The frosting is simply spread on the top of each layer, keeping the sides of the cake open to reveal its gorgeously dark amber color.

Apple Butter–Gingerbread Cake WITH BROWN SUGAR FROSTING

MAKES ONE 9-INCH LAYER CAKE

CAKE

- 2$\frac{3}{4}$ cups all-purpose flour
- $\frac{3}{4}$ cup granulated sugar
- $\frac{1}{4}$ cup packed dark brown sugar
- 2 teaspoons ground ginger
- 1$\frac{1}{2}$ teaspoons ground cinnamon
- 1 teaspoon ground allspice
- 1 teaspoon freshly grated nutmeg
- $\frac{1}{2}$ teaspoon salt
- 1 cup (2 sticks) unsalted butter at room temperature
- 1 cup buttermilk
- 1$\frac{1}{4}$ teaspoons baking soda
- 1 teaspoon vanilla extract
- 5 large eggs
- 1 cup Apple Butter (recipe follows) or store-bought apple butter
- $\frac{1}{2}$ cup finely chopped crystallized ginger

BROWN SUGAR FROSTING

- $\frac{3}{4}$ cup packed dark brown sugar
- $\frac{1}{2}$ cup (1 stick) unsalted butter at room temperature
- 4 cups confectioners' sugar
- $\frac{1}{4}$ teaspoon salt
- $\frac{1}{4}$ cup whole milk
- 1 teaspoon vanilla extract

Position two racks in the middle of the oven and preheat the oven to 350°F. Butter and flour three 9-by-2-inch or 9-by-1-inch round cake pans.

TO MAKE THE CAKE

Combine the flour, granulated and brown sugars, ginger, cinnamon, allspice, nutmeg, and salt in the bowl of an electric mixer fitted with the paddle attachment and begin mixing on medium-low speed. Add the butter, about 2 tablespoons at a time, increase the mixing speed to medium, and continue beating until the mixture resembles the texture of fine bread crumbs. Stir together the buttermilk and baking soda in a small bowl and gradually pour into the beating mixture. Add the vanilla extract and drop in the eggs, one at a time, beating until smooth and

stopping once or twice to scrape the sides of the bowl. Increase the mixing speed to medium-high and beat until light and fluffy. Reduce the speed again to medium and add the Apple Butter and crystallized ginger, mixing just until incorporated.

Divide the batter among the prepared pans and bake for 20 to 25 minutes, or until a wooden skewer inserted in the centers comes out clean. Set the cakes on wire racks to cool in the pans for about 10 minutes before turning out to cool completely.

TO MAKE THE FROSTING

Combine the brown sugar and butter in the bowl of an electric mixer fitted with the paddle attachment and beat on medium-high speed until very light and fluffy. Reduce the mixing speed to low, gradually add the confectioners' sugar and salt, and beat until the mixture is crumbly, stopping once or twice to scrape the sides of the bowl. Pour in the milk and vanilla extract, increase the mixing speed to high, and beat until light and fluffy.

Set one of the cakes on a cake plate and spread one-third of the frosting on top. Repeat the layering process in the same order two more times, finishing with frosting on top.

Serve the cake cut into wedges or about ½-inch-thick square pieces.

Apple Butter

MAKES ABOUT 3 CUPS

3	pounds (about 8 medium) apples (such as Gala or Granny Smith), peeled, cored, and roughly chopped
1	cup apple cider
	Juice of 1 lemon
1	teaspoon grated lemon zest
1¼	cups packed light or dark brown sugar
2	teaspoons ground cinnamon
1	teaspoon ground ginger
¾	teaspoon ground allspice
¼	teaspoon ground cloves
¼	teaspoon salt

Stir together the apples, cider, and lemon juice in a large saucepan. Partially cover the pan and cook over medium-low heat, stirring occasionally, for about 30 minutes, or until the apples are softened.

Purée the cooked apples in a blender, food mill, or in the pan with an immersion blender. Return the purée to the saucepan (if necessary), add the remaining ingredients, and cook over very low heat, stirring occasionally, for about 1½ to 2 hours, or until the apple butter is dark and very thick. The butter is done when pulling a wooden spoon through it creates a distinct path that fills in slowly.

Spoon the hot butter into sterilized jars, seal, and set on a wire rack to cool. Put the butter in the refrigerator for at least several days before using so that the flavors blend and soften. Store the apple butter in the refrigerator for up to 3 months.

Pears and gingerbread make for a perfect match. Each puts us in mind of fall's comforting aromas and flavors, and when combined, the sweet, juicy fruit naturally complements the moist, spicy gingerbread. Perhaps the loveliest thing about upside-down cake is that it can be as informal or dressy a dessert as you wish. Inherently warming and comforting, it is also dazzlingly pretty; this fruited gingerbread is sure to become a new way to enjoy an old favorite.

Spiced Pear Upside-Down Gingerbread Cake

MAKES ONE 9-INCH CAKE

PEARS

- ½ cup packed light brown sugar
- 2 teaspoons ground cinnamon
- 1 teaspoon ground ginger
- 2 tablespoons unsalted butter, melted
- 3 medium Bosc pears, peeled, cored, and cut lengthwise into ¼-inch-thick slices

CAKE

- 1⅓ cups all-purpose flour
- 1 teaspoon salt
- 2 teaspoons baking powder
- ¼ teaspoon baking soda
- 1½ teaspoons ground ginger
- 1½ teaspoons ground cinnamon
- 6 tablespoons unsalted butter at room temperature
- ⅓ cup packed dark brown sugar
- ½ cup molasses
- 1 large egg
- ½ cup whole milk

Vanilla Ice Cream (page 134) for serving (optional)

Position a rack in the middle of the oven and preheat the oven to 350ºF. Butter a 9-by-2-inch round cake pan.

TO PREPARE THE PEARS

Stir together the brown sugar, cinnamon, and ginger in a medium bowl. Spread the melted butter evenly over the bottom of the prepared pan and sprinkle the sugar mixture evenly on top. Arrange the pear slices in a decorative concentric circle pattern over the sugar mixture.

TO MAKE THE CAKE

Whisk together the flour, salt, baking powder, baking soda, ginger, and cinnamon in a large bowl.

Put the butter in the bowl of an electric mixer fitted with the paddle attachment and beat on medium-high speed until smooth. Add the brown sugar and beat until light and fluffy.

Pour in the molasses and beat until smooth. Drop in the egg and mix until incorporated, stopping at least once to scrape the sides of the bowl. Reduce the mixing speed to medium-low and alternately incorporate the flour mixture and milk, beginning and ending with the flour mixture and stopping once or twice to scrape the sides of the bowl. Increase the speed to medium-high and beat until smooth.

Pour the cake batter over the pears and set the pan on a baking sheet. Bake for 40 to 45 minutes, or until the cake is chestnut brown in color and a wooden skewer inserted in the center comes out clean. Set the cake on a wire rack to cool in the pan for 10 to 15 minutes. Run a paring knife around the edges of the cake to loosen them a bit, invert it onto a serving plate, and carefully lift off the pan.

Serve the cake warm or at room temperature cut into wedges and with the Vanilla Ice Cream, if desired.

My maternal grandmother, Adelaide Walls Fighera, had a wicked sweet tooth, but I don't remember her baking much. Ice cream was more her style, as I recall. She did, however, make one annual pilgrimage to the oven. Every Christmas, she baked a rum cake. My mother purchased the ingredients for this cake as we awaited my grandparents' arrival from Florida. The yellow cake mix, butter, a bottle of rum, and chopped walnuts were waiting on the kitchen counter for Mom-Mom when she arrived. We started baking on Christmas Eve. The cake part was pretty straightforward. It was when we prepared the rum syrup, though, that things became a little foggy. When the cake came out of the oven, she began preparing the syrup by melting butter, sugar, and rum in a small pot on the stove. We stirred and tasted, and tasted, and tasted, each time declaring how delicious it was, and improving it every so often with another slosh of rum. By the time we were ready to poke holes in the cake to prepare it for the syrup, we were so full of buttery alcohol that I'm not really sure how we ever succeeded in doing so without skewering ourselves. Somehow I guess we did, though. I can still see the glistening syrup-soaked cake proudly displayed on the sideboard in the dining room. This gingerbread rum cake takes its cue from Mom-Mom's yellow cake–based creation. It is just as rich, buttery, and moist, but it becomes more delicate and fragrant with the addition of nutmeg and ground and crystallized gingers. The rum syrup hasn't changed too much, so proceed with caution as you taste it.

→ Gingerbread Rum Cake ←

MAKES ONE 10-INCH CAKE

CAKE

- 3 cups all-purpose flour
- 2 teaspoons baking powder
- 1 teaspoon salt
- 1 tablespoon ground ginger
- 1/2 teaspoon freshly grated nutmeg
- 1 cup (2 sticks) unsalted butter at room temperature
- 2 cups sugar
- 4 large eggs
- 1 1/2 teaspoons vanilla extract
- 1/2 cup whole milk
- 1/2 cup light or dark rum
- 1/4 cup finely chopped crystallized ginger
- 3/4 cup toasted walnuts, chopped

RUM SYRUP

- 1/4 cup (1/2 stick) unsalted butter
- 1/2 cup sugar
- 6 tablespoons light or dark rum

*

Position a rack in the middle of the oven and preheat the oven to 350°F. Butter and flour a 10-inch tube pan.

TO MAKE THE CAKE

Whisk together the flour, baking powder, salt, ginger, and nutmeg in a large bowl.

Put the butter in the bowl of an electric mixer fitted with the paddle attachment and beat on medium-high speed until smooth. Add the sugar and beat until light and fluffy. Drop in the eggs, one at time, beating until light and smooth and stopping at least once to scrape the sides of the bowl. Stir together the vanilla extract, milk, and rum in a small bowl. Reduce the mixing speed to medium-low and alternately incorporate the flour and milk mixtures, beginning and ending with the flour mixture and stopping once or twice to scrape the sides of the bowl. Add the crystallized ginger and mix just until combined.

Sprinkle the walnuts into the prepared pan, covering the bottom evenly. Pour the batter over the walnuts and bake for about 1 hour, or until the cake is golden brown, the top is cracked, and a wooden skewer inserted near the center comes out clean. Set the cake on a wire rack to cool in the pan for about 15 minutes before turning out to cool for about 10 minutes more, walnut-side up.

MEANWHILE, MAKE THE RUM SYRUP

Combine the butter and sugar in a small saucepan and cook over medium heat, stirring occasionally, until the butter is melted and the sugar is dissolved. Remove from the heat and stir in the rum.

Place a large baking sheet or sheet of aluminum foil under the rack. Using a wooden skewer or toothpick, poke holes all over the top of the cake. (You can poke into the cake about 3 inches or so.) While the cake is still warm, gradually spoon the warm rum syrup over the top, allowing it to drizzle down the sides and absorb into the cake.

Serve the cake warm or at room temperature cut into wedges.

My friend Susan believes that pound cake is the perfect dessert solution for virtually every occasion. She happily fiddles with her pound cake recipe so often, in fact, that she is prepared to share her delicious cakes with lucky and ever-so-appreciative friends and family just about all the time. Susan generously shared the recipe for her moist, buttery creations with me, and these charming mini-Bundt gingerbread cakes are the result of my own tinkering with her master list of ingredients. The cakes are also reminiscent of the golden-colored, delicately spiced gingerbreads that appear in many eighteenth- and nineteenth-century cookery books. Unlike their darker molasses- and treacle-rich counterparts, these early cakes were often sweetened with sugar; spiced with ginger, nutmeg, mace, and caraway seeds; and perfumed with rosewater and citrus. Moist and soft, yet pleasantly dense, this recipe takes well not only to the individual Bundt form, but also to the infusion of warm spices and bright lemon. The syrup, also flavored with ginger and lemon, further flavors the gingerbreads with the vibrant, complementary sensations of heat and tartness. It makes them even more deliciously moist as well. These cakes have little need for additional embellishment. If you'd like, however, a dollop of soft whipped cream pairs with them quite nicely.

Ginger Syrup–Soaked Gingerbread Cakes

MAKES 8 MINI-BUNDT CAKES

CAKES

- 2 cups cake flour
- 1 teaspoon baking powder
- 3/4 teaspoon salt
- 1 tablespoon ground ginger
- 1 teaspoon ground cinnamon
- 1/2 teaspoon freshly grated nutmeg
- 1 cup (2 sticks) unsalted butter at room temperature
- 1 cup sugar
- 3 large eggs
- 6 tablespoons whole milk
  Grated zest of 1 lemon
- 1/2 teaspoon lemon extract or oil
- 1/4 cup finely chopped crystallized ginger
- 2 tablespoons grated peeled fresh ginger

SYRUP

- 1/2 cup sugar
- 1/4 cup water
  Juice of 1 lemon
- 1/3 cup finely chopped peeled fresh ginger

  Whipped Cream (page 132) for serving (optional)

Position a rack in the middle of the oven and preheat the oven to 325ºF. Butter and flour eight 8-ounce mini-Bundt cake cups and set them on a baking sheet. (Mini-Bundt pans usually contain 6 individual cups.)

TO MAKE THE CAKES

Whisk together the cake flour, baking powder, salt, ginger, cinnamon, and nutmeg in a medium bowl.

Put the butter in the bowl of an electric mixer fitted with the paddle attachment and beat on medium-high speed until smooth. Add the sugar and beat until light and fluffy. Drop in

CONTINUED

the eggs, one at time, and beat for about 2 minutes, stopping at least once to scrape the sides of the bowl. Stir together the milk, lemon zest, lemon extract, and crystallized and fresh gingers in a small bowl. Pour the milk mixture into the batter, mixing until combined. Reduce the mixing speed to medium-low and gradually add the flour mixture, beating just until incorporated.

Divide the batter among the prepared Bundt cake cups. Bake for 25 to 30 minutes, or until the cakes are golden brown, puffed, and a wooden skewer inserted near the centers comes out clean.

MEANWHILE, MAKE THE SYRUP

Combine the sugar, water, lemon juice, and ginger in a small saucepan. Bring to a simmer over medium heat, stirring occasionally until the sugar is dissolved. Remove from the heat and set aside, keeping warm.

Set the cakes on a wire rack to cool in the pans for about 10 minutes before turning out onto the rack. Place a large baking sheet or sheet of aluminum foil under the rack. While the cakes are still warm, gradually spoon the warm syrup over the tops, allowing it to absorb completely. Set aside to cool.

Serve the cakes with the Whipped Cream, if desired.

Eighteenth- and early-nineteenth-century recipes often called for liquor, and did so as well in the case of blond gingerbreads. If early cookery books are any indication, sack—a white wine imported from Spain and the Canary Islands—seems to have been quite a popular addition.

Gingerbread and almond cake rank equally high in the category of unpretentious comforting cakes. When the two batters are swirled together into one loaf, the result is a cake that combines the best of both. Each slice is uniquely and prettily marbled with blond and chestnut-colored waves. With each bite, we experience the delicate nuttiness of almond and the complementary gentle warmth of spices and molasses. The cake has a surprisingly soft texture and delicate crumb, so you will want to cut it into generous slices, about 1/2 inch thick. Not too sweet or rich, this cake is as delicious for breakfast or tea as it is for dessert.

Marbled Gingerbread–Almond Loaf Cake

MAKES ONE 9-BY-5-BY-3-INCH LOAF CAKE

1 1/4 cups cake flour
3/4 cup almond flour (almond meal)
2 teaspoons baking powder
1/2 teaspoon salt
1/2 cup (1 stick) unsalted butter at room temperature
3/4 cup granulated sugar
1/4 cup packed light brown sugar

2 large eggs
3/4 cup whole milk
1/2 teaspoon almond extract
1/4 cup dark molasses
1 1/2 teaspoons ground ginger
1 teaspoon ground cinnamon
1/2 teaspoon ground cloves

Position a rack in the middle of the oven and preheat the oven to 350ºF. Butter and flour a 9-by-5-by-3-inch loaf pan.

Whisk together the cake flour, almond flour, baking powder, and salt in a medium bowl.

Put the butter in the bowl of an electric mixer fitted with the paddle attachment and beat on medium-high speed until smooth. Add the granulated and brown sugars and beat until light and fluffy. Drop in the eggs, one at a time, and beat for about 2 minutes, stopping at least once to scrape the sides of the bowl. Reduce the mixing speed to medium-low and alternately incorporate the flour mixture and milk, beginning and ending with the flour mixture and stopping once or twice to scrape the sides of the bowl.

Remove half of the batter to a medium bowl and stir in the almond extract. Stir the molasses, ginger, cinnamon, and cloves into the remaining half of the original batter.

Drop large dollops of each batter into the prepared loaf pan. (This doesn't have to be pretty; haphazard placement is okay.) Using a wooden skewer or paring knife, swirl the batters together to produce a marbled effect. Tap the pan lightly once or twice on the work surface to remove any air bubbles. Bake for 50 to 55 minutes, or until a wooden skewer inserted in the center comes out clean. Set the cake on a wire rack to cool in the pan for 10 to 15 minutes before turning out to cool completely.

Serve the cake cut into thick (about 1/2-inch) slices.

My husband and I were married five days before Christmas. I had already decided I wanted a gingerbread wedding cake when we began talking with renowned pastry chef and friend Robert Bennett. He had kindly offered to prepare the cake for us, and when I suggested including apricot jam, meringue, and praline buttercream between the layers, he happily approved. Needless to say, Robert's cake was the best wedding cake I've ever eaten. It was as stunning as it was delicious, standing four tiers high, covered in seamless white fondant, and decorated with sparkling sugar snowflakes. My version of Robert's inspiring creation includes nearly all of the tasty elements our wedding guests enjoyed. The gingerbread cake is vibrantly spicy, as well as soft and delicate in texture. It's no wonder it marries beautifully with crisp layers of meringue, sweet apricot jam, and velvety smooth buttercream. Decorate the cake with fresh flowers or with piped buttercream rosettes, gold dragées, and colorful coarse sugar, as I have done here. If you wish to celebrate with this cake in the wintertime, as my husband and I did, you might want to spend some extra time making royal icing snowflakes similar to those that decorated our wedding cake. Having prepared this cake once during a summer heat wave, I can tell you that (shocker!) royal icing snowflakes don't like hot weather. In fact, they will downright rebel if you force them to hold their delicate shapes on a humid day. In any event, I have included directions here for making them in case you do want to try your hand at these lacy white lovelies during the cold-weather months they like best.

→ Robert's Celebration Gingerbread Cake ←

MAKES ONE 9-INCH LAYER CAKE

MERINGUE ROUNDS

- 2/3 cup almond flour (almond meal)
- 1 1/2 tablespoons cornstarch
- 1/4 teaspoon salt
- 4 large egg whites (about 1/2 cup)
- 1 cup sugar
- 1/2 teaspoon vanilla extract

CAKE

- 2 1/2 cups all-purpose flour
- 1/2 teaspoon salt
- 1 tablespoon ground ginger
- 2 teaspoons ground cinnamon
- 1 teaspoon ground allspice
- 1 teaspoon ground cloves
- 1/2 teaspoon freshly grated nutmeg
- 1/2 cup (1 stick) unsalted butter at room temperature
- 1/2 cup packed light brown sugar

- 1 cup molasses
- 2 large eggs
- 1/2 cup hot water
- 1/2 cup brewed espresso or strong coffee
- 2 teaspoons baking soda

PRALINE BUTTERCREAM

- 7 cups (1 recipe) Dede's Italian Buttercream (page 135) at room temperature
- 3 tablespoons praline paste

- 1 cup apricot jam or preserves

Orange and pink coarse sanding or decorating sugar for sprinkling (optional)
Gold dragées for decorating (optional)

Royal Icing Snowflakes (recipe follows) for decorating (optional)

CONTINUED

TO MAKE THE MERINGUE ROUNDS

Position a rack in the middle of the oven and preheat the oven to 200°F. Line a large baking sheet with parchment paper. Using a 9-inch round pan, trace two 9-inch circles onto the parchment. Invert the parchment so the markings are on the opposite side but still visible.

Whisk together the almond flour, cornstarch, and salt in a small bowl.

Put the egg whites in the bowl of an electric mixer fitted with the whisk attachment and whip on high speed until frothy. Gradually incorporate the sugar, add the vanilla extract, and whip to stiff, glossy peaks.

Using a rubber spatula, fold in the almond flour mixture, about one-third at a time, working gently but quickly so as not to deflate the meringue. Divide the meringue evenly between the two circles traced onto the parchment, spreading evenly to the edges.

Bake the meringue rounds for about 1 hour, or until they are firm and very light golden brown. Set the meringues on a wire rack to cool completely on the baking sheet.

TO MAKE THE CAKE

Position two racks in the middle of the oven and increase the oven temperature to 350°F. Butter and flour three 9-by-2-inch round cake pans.

Whisk together the flour, salt, ginger, cinnamon, allspice, cloves, and nutmeg in a large bowl.

Put the butter in the bowl of an electric mixer fitted with the paddle attachment and beat on medium-high speed until smooth. Add the brown sugar and beat until light and fluffy. Pour in the molasses and beat until smooth. Drop in the eggs, one at time, mixing until incorporated and stopping at least once to scrape the sides of the bowl. Stir together the hot water, espresso, and baking soda in a small bowl. Reduce the mixing speed to medium-low and alternately incorporate the flour and espresso mixtures, beginning and ending with the flour mixture and stopping once or twice to scrape the sides of the bowl. Increase the mixing speed to medium-high and beat until smooth.

Divide the batter among the prepared pans and bake for 18 to 20 minutes, or until a wooden skewer inserted in the centers comes out clean. Set the gingerbread on wire racks to cool in the pans for about 10 minutes before turning out to cool completely.

TO MAKE THE PRALINE BUTTERCREAM

Put the buttercream in the bowl of an electric mixer fitted with the whisk attachment and whip on medium-high speed until smooth and glossy. Put the praline paste in a medium bowl. Add ½ cup of the buttercream and, using a wire whisk, whip until combined. Whisk in another 2 cups of the buttercream until smooth. Reserve the remaining plain buttercream for frosting the cake.

Place one of the gingerbread cakes on a cake plate (or on a 9-inch cardboard cake round if you plan to move the cake to another platter). Using an icing spatula or wide dinner knife, spread about one-third of the apricot jam over the top. Cover the jam with about one-quarter of the praline buttercream, set a meringue round on top, and spread about another one-quarter of the praline buttercream over it. Spread another one-third of jam over the buttercream and set a second gingerbread cake on top. Continue the layering process with the same quantities in this manner: buttercream, meringue round, buttercream, jam, gingerbread cake.

Cover the cake with a crumb coating of plain buttercream by first putting a dollop of buttercream in the center of the cake. Using an icing spatula or wide dinner knife, spread the butter-cream evenly over the top to the edges. (If it starts to hang over the edges, that's okay, and actually makes the process easier.) Scoop some additional buttercream onto the spatula. Holding it vertically and parallel to the cake with your hand positioned slightly above the top of the cake, spread the buttercream around the sides, scooping up more buttercream as needed.

(This coating is meant to be thin. Don't worry if you can still see the cake layers.) Smooth the ridge that forms around the top edges by holding the spatula horizontally and at a slight angle and carefully swiping it from the edges toward the center of the cake. Set the cake in the refrigerator until the buttercream is fairly firm, about 20 minutes.

Use the same procedure for the crumb coating to cover the chilled cake with a final coating of buttercream, but make the dollop on top a bit bigger and be more generous with the buttercream you scoop onto the spatula to spread around the sides. Don't worry if the cake isn't smooth the first time; keep working with it and add more buttercream until you're satisfied. Reserve about 3/4 cup of the buttercream for the piped decoration. Sprinkle the orange and pink sugar over the top of the cake, if desired. Fill a piping bag fitted with a rosette tip (a Number 24 tip makes a pretty little rosette) with the reserved buttercream. Pipe rosettes of buttercream around the sides and the top edges of the cake and set a gold dragée in the middle of each rosette, if desired. Store any leftover buttercream in an airtight container in the refrigerator for up to 2 weeks or in the freezer for up to 3 months.

Serve the cake cut into about 1/2-inch-thick wedges or square pieces.

Royal Icing Snowflakes

Lemon juice, egg whites, or water for thinning the icing
1 cup Royal Icing (page 136)
Coarse, sanding, or decorating sugar for sprinkling (optional)
Dede's Italian Buttercream for attaching the snowflakes (page 135)

Trace the outline of snowflake cookie cutters onto a sheet of parchment paper. Drizzle enough lemon juice into the royal icing, if necessary, to make the icing thin enough to pipe an outline. (The consistency should resemble rich sour cream. It needs to be thick enough so the snowflakes hold their shapes and resist breaking when dry.) Using a pastry bag fitted with a small round tip (a Number 4 tip is fine here), pipe the icing around the snowflake outlines. Pipe additional lines as you wish to make a lacy design, sprinkle with coarse sugar (if desired), and set aside to dry in a cool, dry area for at least 4 hours or overnight. (The snowflakes will dry more slowly on a hot and even slightly humid day.)

Carefully peel the snowflakes off of the parchment and attach them to the cake, using buttercream.

This cake is named for my mother, not because she prepares it, but, rather, because she can't help but practically inhale it every time I make it. To be honest, I am as fond of fruitcake as she is, and we are both fairly discerning connoisseurs. Not just any fruitcake will do. It has to be warmly spiced with the likes of ginger, cinnamon, nutmeg, and cloves; sweet and dark with brown sugar; and moist with the jewel-colored fruit we like best: raisins, dried cranberries, apricots, dates, prunes, and candied citrus peel. A generous splash of whiskey or rum doesn't hurt, either. As is traditional with fruitcake, we generally like to further contribute to the uninhibited, fervent nature of this cake by dousing it with more of the fiery stuff for at least several weeks after it is baked. It is by no means required, but covering the fruitcake with a smooth, white fondant cloak makes for a lovely finish and presentation. Actually, the cake is first brushed with apricot jam, then covered with a thin sheet of marzipan, and finally enrobed in rolled fondant. These layers not only add flavor and texture, but with the cake stored in a cool area, they help to preserve it for at least three weeks, as well.

→ Carol Lee's Jeweled Gingerbread Fruitcake ←

MAKES ONE 9-INCH CAKE

FRUITCAKE

- 2 cups all-purpose flour
- 1/2 cup almond flour (almond meal)
- 1/2 teaspoon salt
- 2 teaspoons ground ginger
- 1 teaspoon ground cinnamon
- 1/2 teaspoon freshly grated nutmeg
- 1/2 teaspoon ground cloves
- 3 cups dark raisins
- 1 cup golden raisins
- 1 cup dried cranberries
- 1 cup lightly packed dried pitted apricots, chopped
- 1 cup lightly packed dried pitted dates, chopped
- 1/2 cup lightly packed pitted prunes, chopped
- 1/4 cup chopped Candied Orange Peel (page 138) or store-bought candied orange peel
- 1/4 cup chopped Candied Lemon Peel (page 138) or store-bought candied lemon peel

- 1/2 cup whiskey or dark rum, plus more for brushing the baked cake
- 1 cup (2 sticks) unsalted butter at room temperature
- 1 1/4 cups packed dark brown sugar
- 5 large eggs
- 1/4 cup apricot jam or preserves
  Grated zest of 1 lemon
  Grated zest of 1 orange

FINISHES

- 1/3 cup apricot jam or preserves
  Confectioners' sugar for rolling
- 9 to 10 ounces marzipan (available in most supermarkets)
  Cornstarch for rolling
- 1 1/2 pounds rolled fondant (available in craft and cake-decorating stores)
  Silver dragées for decorating (optional)

  Crème Anglaise (page 133) for serving (optional)

Position a rack in the middle of the oven and preheat the oven to 300°F. Butter a 9-by-3-inch springform pan. (A nonstick pan is helpful here.) Line the bottom with a round of parchment, and butter and flour the parchment and sides of the pan.

TO MAKE THE FRUITCAKE

Whisk together the flour, almond flour, salt, ginger, cinnamon, nutmeg, and cloves in a medium bowl. Set aside. Toss together the raisins, cranberries, apricots, dates, prunes, candied orange and lemon peels, and 1/2 cup whiskey in a large bowl.

Put the butter in the bowl of an electric mixer fitted with the paddle attachment and beat on medium-high speed until smooth. Add the brown sugar and beat until light and fluffy. Drop in the eggs, one at time, and beat for about 2 minutes, stopping at least once to scrape down the sides of the bowl. Mix in the jam and the lemon and orange zests. Reduce the mixing speed to medium-low and gradually add the flour mixture, beating just until incorporated. Add the dried fruit mixture, about one-quarter at a time, mixing just until the fruit is evenly distributed throughout the batter.

Pour the batter into the prepared pan. Wrap the pan with a parchment collar that rises about 3 inches above the pan and secure with kitchen twine. Set the filled pan on a baking sheet and bake for about 2 hours, or until the cake is dark chestnut brown in color, the top is slightly cracked, and a wooden skewer inserted in the center comes out clean (a few sticky crumbs are okay, too).

Set the cake on a wire rack to cool for about 30 minutes in the pan before turning out to cool completely. Brush with whiskey (about 1/4 cup will do for now) and wrap the fruitcake in plastic wrap. Store the cake for at least 3 weeks in an airtight container, dousing it with about 1/4 cup of whiskey at least once a week. You can serve the cake at this point or proceed with the method for covering the cake with fondant.

TO FINISH THE FRUITCAKE

Set the cake on a parchment-lined baking sheet. (If you find that the top of the cake is very bumpy, invert the cake so the smooth side faces up. A slightly lumpy top has never really bothered me, though.) Push the apricot jam through a strainer into a small bowl to remove the apricot bits and discard them. Brush the jam all over the cake. Lightly dust a work surface with confectioners' sugar, roll the marzipan to about 1/16 inch thick (very thin), and cut out a 14-inch-diameter circle. Carefully roll the marzipan over the rolling pin and unroll it on top of the fruitcake, smoothing it over the top and down the sides to remove any air bubbles or bumps. Trim any excess marzipan from the bottom of the cake to make a clean edge.

Clean the work surface and lightly dust it with cornstarch. Roll the fondant to 1/4 inch thick and cut out a 14-inch-diameter circle. Carefully pick up the fondant circle from underneath with both hands as though carrying a tray (you can't roll the fondant, as it will stick to itself). Place the fondant over the marzipan-covered fruitcake, again smoothing the top and sides. Trim any excess fondant from the bottom of the cake to make a clean edge. If desired, cut decorative shapes out of the remaining fondant, dampen with water, and apply onto the covered cake. Finish by pressing silver dragées (if desired) into the fondant.

Serve the cake immediately cut into thin wedges or squares with Crème Anglaise, if desired. To store the cake, wrap it in plastic wrap and set it in the refrigerator or in a cool, dry area for up to 3 weeks.

This gingerbread is, as you can guess, a cross between an old-fashioned chocolate cake and a traditional spicy gingerbread. Properly mixing ingredients is particularly important for this gingerbread, given that the batter is so rich in sugar, molasses, and chocolate. Employing the two-stage method is best here. This is an easy procedure in which the dry ingredients are combined, the butter is incorporated, and then the liquid and eggs are beaten into the batter until it is smooth and light. The result is cake that is not only rich and complex in flavor, but also surprisingly delicate, tender, and comfortingly moist.

Rich Chocolate Gingerbread

MAKES ONE 9-INCH CAKE

4 ounces semisweet or bittersweet chocolate, chopped
$1/2$ cup Dutch-process cocoa powder
$1^1/2$ cups hot water
$2^1/4$ cups cake flour
1 cup packed dark brown sugar
1 teaspoon baking soda
1 teaspoon baking powder
$1/2$ teaspoon salt
2 teaspoons ground ginger

$1^1/2$ teaspoons ground cinnamon
$1/4$ teaspoon freshly grated nutmeg
$1/4$ teaspoon ground cloves
$3/4$ cup ($1^1/2$ sticks) unsalted butter at room temperature
$1^1/2$ teaspoons vanilla extract
3 large eggs
1 cup molasses

Vanilla Ice Cream (page 134) for serving (optional)

Position a rack in the middle of the oven and preheat the oven to 350°F. Butter and flour a 9-by-2-inch square baking pan.

Put the chocolate in a small, heatproof bowl. Set the bowl over a saucepan filled with about $1^1/2$ inches of simmering water (being sure not to let the bottom of the bowl touch the water) and stir occasionally until the chocolate is melted and smooth. Remove the bowl from the saucepan and set aside to cool slightly, about 10 minutes. (You can also melt the chocolate in the microwave, heating it at about 20-second intervals and stirring periodically until it is melted and smooth.)

Whisk together the cocoa powder and hot water in a medium bowl until smooth.

Combine the cake flour, brown sugar, baking soda, baking powder, salt, ginger, cinnamon, nutmeg, and cloves in the bowl of an electric mixer fitted with the paddle attachment and begin mixing on medium-low speed. Add the butter, about 2 tablespoons at a time, increase the mixing speed to medium, and continue beating until the mixture resembles the texture of fine bread crumbs. Pour in the cocoa liquid and mix until combined. Add the vanilla extract and drop in the eggs, one at a time, beating until smooth and stopping once or twice to scrape the sides of the bowl. Pour in the molasses and the melted chocolate, increase the mixing speed to medium-high, and beat until smooth, about 30 seconds.

Pour the batter into the prepared pan and bake for about 55 minutes, or until a wooden skewer inserted in the center comes out clean (a few sticky crumbs are okay, too). Set the cake on a wire rack to cool almost completely in the pan.

Serve the gingerbread cut into squares and with the Vanilla Ice Cream, if desired.

In 1828, renowned cookery book author Eliza Leslie published what arguably became her most celebrated work, *Seventy-Five Receipts for Pastry, Cakes, and Sweetmeats*. Three gingerbread recipes appear in this volume: Gingerbread Nuts, Common Gingerbread, and Lafayette Gingerbread. Typical of this period, Leslie included all of these recipes in her Cakes chapter. Only the Lafayette version, however, resembles modern-day cake, while the author instructed the others (cookies, really) to be rolled into balls and cut into shapes. My version of Lafayette gingerbread takes its cue from Miss Leslie's. Robust and sweet with molasses and brown sugar; spicy with a good dose of ginger, cinnamon, allspice, and cloves; and bright with the freshness of lemon, this simple cake is moist and satisfying. Lafayette gingerbread is certainly elegant enough to serve plain. I do believe, however, Miss Leslie would have approved of accompanying squares of this dark cake with shiny, sugary preserved apricots and/or a drizzle of velvety crème anglaise.

→ Eliza Leslie's Lafayette Gingerbread ←

MAKES ONE 9-INCH CAKE

2½ cups all-purpose flour
½ teaspoon salt
1 tablespoon ground ginger
2 teaspoons ground cinnamon
1 teaspoon ground allspice
1 teaspoon ground cloves
½ cup (1 stick) unsalted butter at room temperature
½ cup packed dark brown sugar

1 cup molasses
2 large eggs
2 teaspoons baking soda
1 cup hot water
Juice and grated zest of 1 lemon

Preserved Apricots (page 118) for serving (optional)
Crème Anglaise (page 133) for serving (optional)

Position a rack in the middle of the oven and preheat the oven to 350ºF. Butter and flour a 9-by-3-inch springform pan.

Whisk together the flour, salt, ginger, cinnamon, allspice, and cloves in a large bowl.

Put the butter in the bowl of an electric mixer fitted with the paddle attachment and beat on medium-high speed until smooth. Add the brown sugar and beat until light and fluffy. Pour in the molasses and beat until smooth. Drop in the eggs, one at time, and mix until incorporated, stopping at least once to scrape the sides of the bowl. Dissolve the baking soda in the hot water in a small bowl. Reduce the mixing speed to medium-low and alternately incorporate the flour mixture and baking soda mixture, beginning and ending with the flour mixture and

stopping once or twice to scrape the sides of the bowl. Add the lemon juice and zest and beat just until incorporated.

Pour the batter into the prepared pan and bake for about 45 minutes, or until the cake is dark chestnut brown in color, the top is cracked, and a wooden skewer inserted in the center comes out clean. Set the gingerbread on a wire rack to cool in the pan for about 10 minutes before turning out to cool for about 10 minutes more.

Serve the cake warm or at room temperature cut into squares and with the Preserved Apricots and/or a drizzle of the Crème Anglaise, if desired.

Just exactly why Miss Leslie named this recipe for the Marquis de Lafayette isn't entirely clear. We know that he made his third and final visit to America in 1824, staying for nearly a year and a half, and passing through a number of cities, including New York, Philadelphia, and Baltimore. Miss Leslie was no doubt aware of this, and perhaps his appearance had some influence on the recipes she was creating at the time.

Another theory proposes that Leslie's recipe refers to an actual encounter between Lafayette and gingerbread. The colorful annals relating to George Washington's mother, Mary Ball Washington, suggest that when the marquis visited her at her home on Charles Street in Fredericksburg, Virginia, she hosted him with a mint julep and gingerbread. Mrs. Washington had been living in town since moving from her farm in 1772. The marquis returned to America for a second time in 1780, so perhaps it was then that the president took him to visit his mother. Eliza Leslie was only a child at this time. Years later, though, during his third visit to America, he passed again through Fredericksburg, this time to pay respects to Mrs. Washington's gravesite in 1825. Maybe Leslie learned of the gingerbread story then, and decided to add it to her collection of soon-to-be-published recipes.

This gingerbread must have been rich and spicy indeed. For "A pound and a half of flour," Miss Leslie called for "Five eggs . . . Half a pound of brown sugar . . . Half a pound of butter . . . A pint of sugar-house molasses . . . Four tablespoonfuls of ginger . . . Two large sticks of cinnamon . . . Three dozen grains of allspice . . . [and] Three dozen of cloves . . . powdered and sifted." A good dose of lemon—"The juice and grated peel of two large lemons"—surely added a bit of refreshing tartness and moisture to the cake, which Miss Leslie noted was "the finest of all gingerbread."

In my opinion, the cookie jar should be filled with gingerbread cookies year-round. Hard and crisp, soft and chewy, or moist and cakelike, these sweet and spicy gems fill the house with warming aromas and satisfy our cravings in ways that only homemade cookies can.

CHAPTER TWO: Cookies

Gingerbread cookies date back many centuries. As early as the Middle Ages, European bakers pressed thick, honey-sweetened spice dough into decorative molds. Communities used these dense cakes to commemorate holidays and celebrations, and the images varied widely depending on the occasion. Flowers and religious symbols, in fact, seem to have been as popular as royal figures and even quite bawdy, scantily clad lovers. These flat spice cakes took simpler cutout or molded forms as well. By the eighteenth century, these more modest-looking gingerbreads were as popular as their fancier medieval predecessors. Many were rich with dark treacle, molasses, or honey and flavored with a variety of spices. Others, however, were lighter in color and perhaps more delicate in flavor. Sweetened with sugar, they were often spiced primarily with ginger and perfumed with citrus or rosewater. Our penchant for gingerbread cookies remains as strong as it was centuries ago. What could be more deliciously old-fashioned than a crisp, crinkle-topped gingersnap? On the other hand, soft molasses cookies are seductively moist and chewy. And super-moist, ginger-scented brownies are a slightly exotic, grown-up form of the plain chocolate variety we enjoyed as kids. Spice up your cookie jar and make a batch of gingerbread cookies. Whether you bake up a familiar recipe or try a new one, your cookie cravings are sure to be satisfied.

For years I have been searching for a satisfying gingersnap recipe. I have spent many hours searching through cookbooks, recipe pamphlets, and magazines, hungry for that perfect combination of crisp, sweet, spicy goodness. Happily, I have finally discovered a successful recipe. It delivers a consistently satisfying gingersnap complete with the mandatory crunch and gingery sweetness we crave from a traditional cookie. This recipe comes together quickly and, in keeping with its old-fashioned simplicity, is best prepared by hand (no electric mixer required). The batter will also keep for a day or so in the refrigerator in case you don't wish to bake all of the cookies at once. To my mind, these little rounds are gingersnap perfection. They will, however, spoil you silly. To be sure, no store-bought ginger cookie will ever satisfy you again once you've crunched on these luscious morsels.

→ Old-Time Gingersnaps ←

MAKES ABOUT 30 COOKIES

2 cups all-purpose flour
2 teaspoons baking soda
$1/2$ teaspoon salt
2 teaspoons ground ginger
$1^1/2$ teaspoons ground cinnamon

$3/4$ teaspoon ground cloves
$3/4$ cup ($1^1/2$ sticks) unsalted butter, melted and cooled
1 cup sugar, plus more for rolling
$1/4$ cup molasses
1 large egg

Whisk together the flour, baking soda, salt, ginger, cinnamon, and cloves in a medium bowl.

Combine the butter, 1 cup sugar, and molasses in a large bowl and stir until combined. Drop in the egg, mixing until incorporated. Gradually stir in the flour mixture, mixing to form a soft dough. Cover with plastic wrap and set in the refrigerator to chill for at least 2 hours or overnight.

Position a rack in the middle of the oven and preheat the oven to 350°F. Line baking sheets with parchment paper.

Shape the dough into walnut-size balls, roll in sugar, and arrange them about 2 inches apart on the prepared baking sheets. (If your kitchen is quite warm and the dough balls become soft, set them in the refrigerator until chilled and fairly firm.) Bake for 10 to 12 minutes, or until the cookies have spread, are light golden brown, and the cracks still appear moist.

Cool the cookies on the baking sheets set on wire racks for about 1 minute before removing them to the racks to cool completely. Store the cookies in an airtight container or in a zip-top bag for up to 4 days.

Chinese five-spice powder is an aromatic mixture of spices used widely in Chinese cooking. It might seem a bit unusual adding it to gingersnaps, but really, you need only the littlest bit. Usually containing equal parts of cinnamon, cloves, star anise, fennel seed, and Szechuan peppercorns, the sweet and pungent spices combine with the ginger to give these cookies an exotic aroma and flavor. In addition, the recipe's fairly generous amount of butter seems to have a calming effect on these vibrant spices. Once they are well lubricated in the dough, the five-spice powder and ginger seem to soften and become more delicate, thus suiting this sweet application even more deliciously. These gingersnaps distinguish themselves not only in flavor, but also in texture. Crisp but ever so slightly tender, they accompany a cup of black Lapsang Souchong tea as well as they do a cold glass of milk.

Five-Spice Gingersnaps

MAKES ABOUT 50 COOKIES

3 cups all-purpose flour
1½ teaspoons baking soda
½ teaspoon salt
2¼ teaspoons Chinese five-spice powder
¼ teaspoon ground ginger

1 cup (2 sticks) unsalted butter at room temperature
1¾ cups sugar, plus more for rolling
½ cup heavy (whipping) cream
⅓ cup molasses
1½ teaspoons apple cider vinegar

Whisk together the flour, baking soda, salt, Chinese five-spice powder, and ginger in a medium bowl.

Put the butter in the bowl of an electric mixer fitted with the paddle attachment and beat on medium-high speed until smooth. Add the 1¾ cups sugar and continue beating until incorporated. The mixture will be a bit grainy and clumpy, not light and fluffy. Stir together the cream, molasses, and vinegar in a small bowl. Reduce the mixing speed to medium-low and pour in the cream and molasses mixture, stopping at least once to scrape the sides of the bowl. The mixture might appear a bit lumpy at this point. Gradually add the flour mixture, mixing until just incorporated. Scrape the dough into a large bowl, cover with plastic wrap, and set in the refrigerator to chill for at least 2 hours or overnight.

Position a rack in the middle of the oven and preheat the oven to 350°F. Line baking sheets with parchment paper.

Shape the dough into walnut-size balls, roll in sugar, and arrange them 2 to 3 inches apart on the prepared baking sheets. Bake for 13 to 15 minutes, or until the cookies have spread, are light golden brown, and the tops are cracked.

Cool the cookies on the baking sheets set on wire racks for about 2 minutes before removing them to the racks to cool completely. Store the cookies in an airtight container or in a zip-top bag for up to 5 days.

For at least six centuries, bakers have been decorating spice cookies by pressing them into wooden or ceramic molds. The images they bore varied widely. Some were naturalistic, displaying the likes of flowers and birds. Religious icons and royal figures were also popular. Other designs were used to celebrate weddings, births, and holidays, and some figurative molds are known to have been quite bawdy. (Wonder what they celebrated.) Fortunately, wooden and resin molds of many sizes and designs are available in a variety of kitchenware stores. This sweet and spicy gingerbread dough works in just about any mold. Your yield will, of course, depend on the size of mold you use, and you will probably need to adjust the baking time if your molds are much bigger than the size I suggest. Pressed cookies are pretty and easy alternatives to decorated cookies around the holidays. They make great homemade ornaments, too.

→ Pressed Spicy Gingerbread Cookies ←
MAKES ABOUT FORTY-EIGHT 2-INCH COOKIES

3 cups all-purpose flour
$3/4$ teaspoon salt
$1/4$ teaspoon baking soda
1 tablespoon ground ginger
2 teaspoons ground cinnamon
1 teaspoon ground cloves

$3/4$ teaspoon ground mace
$1/2$ teaspoon mustard powder
$1/2$ cup (1 stick) unsalted butter at room temperature
$1/4$ cup packed dark brown sugar
$3/4$ cup molasses

Whisk together the flour, salt, baking soda, ginger, cinnamon, cloves, mace, and mustard powder in a medium bowl.

Put the butter in the bowl of an electric mixer fitted with the paddle attachment and beat on medium-high speed until smooth. Add the brown sugar and continue beating until light and fluffy. Pour in the molasses and beat until smooth. Gradually add the flour mixture, stopping at least once to scrape the sides of the bowl, and mix just until the dough comes together. Turn the dough out onto a large sheet of plastic wrap, shape into a disc, and wrap tightly. Set in the refrigerator to chill for at least 30 minutes.

Position a rack in the middle of the oven and preheat the oven to 350°F. Line baking sheets with parchment paper.

Break off golf ball–size pieces of the chilled dough, dust them lightly with flour, and press into the molds. The pieces should be big enough for each pressed cookie to measure between $3/16$ and $1/4$ inch thick. You can also use a rolling pin to further flatten the surface, if necessary. To remove each cookie, hold the filled mold perpendicular to the work surface and whack the edge of the mold firmly against it. If the cookie doesn't fall out by itself, carefully loosen the edges with your fingers. Arrange the cookies at least $11/2$ inches apart on the prepared baking sheets and set in the refrigerator until chilled and firm, about 15 minutes.

Using a paring knife, trim the edges of the cookies, if necessary, to make them look as neat and even as possible. Bake for about 10 minutes, or until the cookies are light golden brown and firm.

Cool the cookies on the baking sheets set on wire racks for about 2 minutes before removing them to the racks to cool completely. Store the cookies in an airtight container or in a zip-top bag for up to 2 weeks.

When I was a child, we used to buy Moravian ginger cookies packaged in red cylindrical tins from a local gourmet shop at Christmastime. They were so thin and crisp that I marveled at how these delicate cookies could also pack such a punch of flavor. I have spent a long while searching for a recipe that resembles the cookies I enjoyed years ago. Too often, my attempts resulted in greasy or crumbly rounds that were also lackluster in flavor. Finally, I hit on a recipe that produces spicy, sweet, and really, really crisp little gems. What's more, the dough is easy to prepare and keeps well in the refrigerator for weeks. The key to these cookies is to roll the dough very thin. Yes, this requires a bit of patience, but the results are worth any sore knuckles you might incur during the rolling process. Cut the dough into any shape you like. Just know that smaller cookies rolled this thin are easier to remove from the work surface than larger ones. Be careful, too, and watch the cookies carefully during baking, as they turn from perfectly crisp delights to burned shards very quickly.

Moravian Ginger Thins

MAKES ABOUT SIXTY-FOUR 4-INCH STAR COOKIES, OR ABOUT EIGHTY 2½-INCH ROUND COOKIES

1¾ cups all-purpose flour
¾ teaspoon baking soda
½ teaspoon salt
1½ teaspoons ground cinnamon
1½ teaspoons ground ginger
1½ teaspoons ground cloves
½ teaspoon freshly grated nutmeg

¼ cup (½ stick) unsalted butter at room temperature
⅓ cup packed dark brown sugar
½ cup molasses, warmed
2 tablespoons Grand Marnier or whiskey
¼ teaspoon orange extract or orange oil
¾ teaspoon orange flower water

Whisk together the flour, baking soda, salt, cinnamon, ginger, cloves, and nutmeg in a medium bowl.

Put the butter in the bowl of an electric mixer fitted with the paddle attachment and mix on medium-high speed until smooth. Add the brown sugar and continue beating until light and fluffy. Pour in the molasses and mix until smooth. Drizzle in the Grand Marnier, orange extract, and orange flower water, mixing until incorporated. Reduce the mixing speed to low and gradually incorporate the flour mixture, mixing just until the dough comes together. Turn the dough out onto a large sheet of plastic wrap, shape into a disc, and wrap tightly. Set in the refrigerator to chill for at least 3 hours or overnight.

Position a rack in the middle of the oven and preheat the oven to 325°F. Line baking sheets with parchment paper.

Using about one-quarter of the chilled dough at a time, and keeping the remainder refrigerated, roll the dough on a lightly floured work surface as thin as possible (nearly paper thin), at least ¹⁄₁₆ inch thick. Using a 4-inch star cutter (or other desired shape), cut the dough and carefully arrange about 1 inch apart on the prepared baking sheets.

Bake for about 7 minutes, or until the cookies are crisp and golden brown. They will go from just right to too dark very quickly, so watch them carefully.

Cool the cookies on the baking sheets set on wire racks for about 2 minutes before removing them to the racks to cool completely. Store the cookies in an airtight container or in a zip-top bag for up to 1 week. Store the dough in the refrigerator for up to 5 days or in the freezer for up to 1 month.

What are the holidays without cutout gingerbread cookies? I know from firsthand experience, however, that nearly every-one dreads the work involved making them. First, many recipes yield a large and unwieldy quantity of dough—one that every little hand (if you have them around) wants to grab and consume. Then there's the laborious rolling and cutting involved. Flour ends up everywhere but on the work surface, and piles of cookies quickly build up in every corner of the kitchen. Finally, there's the decorating. It's messy, complicated, and enough of a hassle that we wonder why we didn't just buy those sausage-like rolls of refrigerated cut-and-bake dough from the supermarket. Well, in the spirit of the holidays (or any other happy day of the year you wish to make these cookies), I say everyone just relax a minute. The good news is that this recipe comes together easily, makes a manageable amount of dough, and the cookies are delicious enough to serve plain or with very simple royal icing decoration. Because there is no egg in this dough, cautious mommies also don't have to worry about little ones grabbing and nibbling bits of it. This dough is fairly smooth and easy to work with, as well, so rolling it out requires little work or anxiety. To make the job even easier, roll small amounts of dough at a time and keep the remainder in the refrigerator. This will help the cookies maintain their shapes in the oven. This recipe is flexible, too. You can make the cookies thick and chewy or thin and crisp, depending on how you like them. Finally, decorate the baked cookies by simply spreading them with thick royal icing, or thin the icing and pipe it in as detailed a manner as you wish. Once you have this recipe under your apron belt, you'll never consider buying sausage-shaped cookie dough again.

⇢ Cutout Gingerbread Cookies ⇠

MAKES FIFTEEN 5-INCH COOKIES

$3^{1}/_{2}$ cups all-purpose flour
1 teaspoon baking soda
$3/_{4}$ teaspoon salt
1 tablespoon ground cinnamon
1 tablespoon ground ginger
$3/_{4}$ teaspoon ground cloves
$1/_{2}$ teaspoon ground allspice

$3/_{4}$ cup ($1^{1}/_{2}$ sticks) unsalted butter at room temperature
$1/_{2}$ cup packed light brown sugar
1 cup molasses
$1/_{4}$ cup heavy (whipping) cream
3 cups (1 recipe) Royal Icing (page 136), or as needed (optional)
Lemon juice, egg whites, or water for thinning the icing

Whisk together the flour, baking soda, salt, cinnamon, ginger, cloves, and allspice in a large bowl.

Put the butter in the bowl of an electric mixer fitted with the paddle attachment and beat on medium-high speed until smooth. Add the brown sugar and beat until light and fluffy. Pour in the molasses and beat until smooth, stopping once or twice to scrape the sides of the bowl. Reduce the mixing speed to low and gradually incorporate the flour mixture. Pour in the cream, mixing just until the dough comes together. Turn the

dough out onto a large sheet of plastic wrap, shape into a disc or rectangle, and wrap tightly. Set in the refrigerator to chill for at least 2 hours or overnight.

Position a rack in the middle of the oven and preheat the oven to 350°F. Line baking sheets with parchment paper.

Roll the dough on a lightly floured work surface to about $1/_{4}$ inch thick and, using gingerbread-people cookie cutters, cut into large (about 5-by-$4^{1}/_{4}$-inch) gingerbread boys or girls (or other

CONTINUED

desired shapes). Arrange the cookies about 1½ inches apart on the prepared baking sheets.

Bake for 8 to 10 minutes, or until the cookies are firm around the edges but are still slightly soft in the centers. (See Note for baking thin cookies.)

Cool the cookies on the baking sheets set on wire racks for about 2 minutes before removing them to the racks to cool completely.

Decorate the cookies, if desired, thinning the royal icing with lemon juice as needed. Set them aside in a cool area to dry completely, for 1 to 4 hours, depending on the weather. (If it's rainy or particularly humid, the icing will require a longer drying time.) Store the cookies in an airtight container or in a zip-top bag for up to 4 days.

NOTE

For thin and crisp cookies, preheat the oven to 325ºF. Roll the dough to about 1/8 inch thick, and bake the cookies for about 15 minutes, or until they are crisp at the edges and firm in the centers. Cool the cookies in the same manner.

Although I am crazy for dark, spicy, molasses-rich gingerbread cookies, I wanted to create a cutout version that was a bit more delicate in flavor. These goodies are sweetened with honey rather than molasses, which lends a delightful floral note to the cookies. In addition, the combination of granulated and brown sugars results in a golden treat that is comfortingly soft, but also maintains its shape in the oven. You can bake these cookies plain or sprinkled with sugar. Alternatively, once they have cooled, you can decorate them with royal icing for a twist on traditional gingerbread cutouts.

Golden Gingerbread Cutout Cookies

MAKES ABOUT TWENTY 4-INCH COOKIES

2 cups all-purpose flour
1/2 teaspoon salt
1/4 teaspoon baking soda
2 teaspoons ground ginger
1 1/2 teaspoons ground cinnamon
1/2 teaspoon ground cloves
1/4 teaspoon freshly grated nutmeg
1/4 teaspoon ground allspice
1/2 cup (1 stick) unsalted butter at room temperature

1/4 cup granulated sugar
1/4 cup packed light brown sugar
1/4 cup honey
1 large egg

3 cups (1 recipe) Royal Icing (page 136), or as needed (optional)
Lemon juice, egg whites, or water for thinning the icing

*

Whisk together the flour, salt, baking soda, ginger, cinnamon, cloves, nutmeg, and allspice in a medium bowl.

Put the butter in the bowl of an electric mixer fitted with the paddle attachment and beat on medium-high speed until smooth. Add the granulated and brown sugars and continue beating until light and fluffy. Pour in the honey and beat until smooth. Drop in the egg, mixing until incorporated and stopping once or twice to scrape the sides of the bowl. Reduce the mixing speed to low and gradually add the flour mixture, mixing just until the dough comes together. The dough will be very soft. Turn the dough out onto a large sheet of plastic wrap, press into a disc, and wrap tightly. Set in the refrigerator to chill for at least 2 hours or overnight.

Position a rack in the middle of the oven and preheat the oven to 350°F. Line baking sheets with parchment paper.

Roll the dough on a well-floured work surface to about 1/4 inch thick and cut into 4-inch cookies (or other desired sizes). Arrange the cookies about 2 inches apart on the prepared baking sheets and bake for 8 to 10 minutes, or until they are golden brown.

Cool the cookies on the baking sheets set on wire racks for about 2 minutes before removing them to the racks to cool completely.

Decorate the cookies, if desired, thinning the royal icing with lemon juice as needed. Set aside in a cool area to dry completely, for 1 to 4 hours, depending on the weather. (If it's rainy or particularly humid, the icing will require a longer drying time.) Store the cookies in an airtight container or in a zip-top bag for up to 1 week.

Sometimes we get lucky in baking and hit on a recipe that works wonderfully the first time we make it. Such was the case with these cookies. Elegantly thin, super-crisp, and fragrant with maple and spice, they were not only pretty, but flavorful as well. There is no molasses or brown sugar in these gingerbread cookies. Rather, a mixture of granulated sugar and golden syrup (also known in Britain as light treacle) gives them a mellow, somehow comforting, sweetness that complements the generous amount of spice in the dough. Admittedly, this recipe makes a lot of cookies. I used a relatively small maple leaf-shaped cutter here, but you can certainly use a bigger cutter and make fewer cookies, if you wish. The dough keeps pretty well for a few days in the refrigerator, too, so you actually don't have to make a lot of cookies all at once. The most important thing is to roll the dough very thin, about 1/16 inch thick. This will ensure crisp, delicate cookies that break easily when you bite into them. Finally, sprinkling them with coarse or decorating sugar before baking isn't necessary, but it is a nice touch. The cookies not only shimmer (as the name implies), but the sugar also adds a pleasant bit of a crunchy texture, too.

→ Shimmering Gingerbread Maple Leaves ←
MAKES ONE HUNDRED 2½-BY-3-INCH COOKIES

3¼ cups all-purpose flour
1¼ teaspoons baking soda
¾ teaspoon salt
1 tablespoon ground cinnamon
1½ teaspoons ground ginger
1 cup (2 sticks) unsalted butter at room temperature

1⅓ cups granulated sugar
2 tablespoons golden syrup (such as Lyle's Golden Syrup)
1 teaspoon maple extract
1 large egg
Coarse, sanding, or decorating sugar for sprinkling

Whisk together the flour, baking soda, salt, cinnamon, and ginger in a large bowl.

Put the butter in the bowl of an electric mixer fitted with the paddle attachment and beat on medium-high speed until smooth. Add the granulated sugar and continue beating until light and fluffy. Pour in the golden syrup and beat until smooth. Add the maple extract and drop in the egg, mixing until incorporated and stopping once or twice to scrape the sides of the bowl. Reduce the mixing speed to low and gradually add the flour mixture, mixing just until the dough comes together. Turn the dough out onto a large sheet of plastic wrap, shape into a disc, and wrap tightly. Set in the refrigerator to chill at least 2 hours or overnight.

Position a rack in the middle of the oven and preheat the oven to 350°F. Line baking sheets with parchment paper.

Using about one-quarter to one-third of the dough at a time and refrigerating the remainder, roll the dough on a lightly floured work surface to about 1/16 inch thick (very thin). Cut the dough into leaves, using a 2½-by-3-inch leaf-shaped cutter (or other desired cutter). Arrange the cookies about 1 inch apart on the prepared baking sheets and sprinkle with coarse sugar.

Bake for 8 to 10 minutes, or until the cookies are golden brown, crisp, and fragrant.

Cool the cookies on the baking sheets set on wire racks for about 2 minutes before removing them to the racks to cool completely. Store the cookies in an airtight container or in a zip-top bag for up to 4 days.

There is something magical about chocolate crinkle cookies. Little balls of dark chocolate dough are cloaked in a generous coating of confectioners' sugar and lined up in neat rows on a baking sheet. Then, once in the oven, they are transformed, breaking through the protective white powder and organized line-ups, spreading and cracking as they please. These wondrously crisp and chewy medallions are not only beautiful, but they pack a powerful chocolate punch, as well. This recipe is a play on the traditional chocolate crinkle cookie. The generous infusion of powdered and crystallized gingers gives the cookie a spicy wallop that excitingly enhances and intensifies the chocolate experience.

Chocolate-Ginger Crinkle Cookies

MAKES 40 COOKIES

$^3/_4$ cup all-purpose flour
$^1/_4$ cup Dutch-process cocoa powder
 1 teaspoon baking powder
$^1/_2$ teaspoon salt
$1^1/_2$ teaspoons ground ginger
 1 teaspoon ground cinnamon
$^1/_2$ cup (1 stick) unsalted butter at room temperature

$7^1/_2$ ounces bittersweet or semisweet chocolate, chopped
$^3/_4$ cup granulated sugar
$^1/_4$ cup packed dark brown sugar
 2 large eggs
 1 teaspoon vanilla extract
$^1/_4$ cup finely chopped crystallized ginger
    Confectioners' sugar for rolling

Whisk together the flour, cocoa powder, baking powder, salt, ginger, and cinnamon in a medium bowl.

Combine the butter and 3 ounces of the chocolate in a medium, heatproof bowl. Set the bowl over a saucepan filled with about $1^1/_2$ inches of simmering water (being sure not to let the bottom of the bowl touch the water) and stir occasionally until the chocolate and butter have melted and the mixture is smooth. Remove the bowl from the saucepan and set aside to cool slightly, about 10 minutes. (You can also melt the mixture in the microwave, heating it at about 20-second intervals and stirring periodically until it is melted and smooth.)

Stir the granulated and brown sugars into the melted chocolate mixture, using a wooden spoon or heatproof spatula. Drop in the eggs, one at a time, mixing briskly until smooth. Stir in the vanilla extract and gradually incorporate the flour mixture. Fold in the remaining $4^1/_2$ ounces of chocolate and the crystallized ginger. Cover the dough with plastic wrap and set in the refrigerator to chill for at least 2 hours or overnight.

Position a rack in the middle of the oven and preheat the oven to 350°F. Line baking sheets with parchment paper.

Shape the chilled dough into walnut-size balls, roll in confectioners' sugar, and arrange them about 2 inches apart on the prepared baking sheets. (If your kitchen is quite warm and the dough becomes too soft, return it to the refrigerator until chilled and fairly firm.) Bake for 10 to 12 minutes, or until the cookies have spread and the tops are cracked.

Cool the cookies on the baking sheets set on wire racks for about 2 minutes before removing them to the racks to cool completely. Store the cookies in an airtight container or in a zip-top bag for up to 4 days.

These gorgeous, slightly oversize cookies are sumptuously soft and chewy. As they bake, the cookies spread, developing gooey craters, which break through the glittery, sugary surface. Time, of course, is crucial here. Watch the cookies carefully and whisk them out of the oven as soon as you see that the edges are golden, but the cracks and craters still appear moist. If you prefer a slightly firmer cookie, just leave them in the oven for a minute or two longer. These cookies are delicious on their own or with a glass of milk. Because they are neither too soft nor too crisp, they also serve as the perfect edible framework in an ice cream sandwich. Pair them with your favorite ice cream or use them to prepare Gingerbread-Pumpkin Ice Cream Sandwiches (page 77).

→ Giant Chewy Ginger Cookies ←

MAKES ABOUT 24 COOKIES

2¼ cups all-purpose flour
2 teaspoons baking soda
¼ teaspoon salt
1½ teaspoons ground cinnamon
1½ teaspoons ground ginger
½ teaspoon ground allspice
¼ teaspoon freshly grated nutmeg

¼ teaspoon ground cloves
¾ cup (1½ sticks) unsalted butter at room temperature
1 cup packed light brown sugar
⅓ cup molasses
1 tablespoon finely chopped crystallized ginger
1 large egg
Granulated sugar for rolling

Whisk together the flour, baking soda, salt, cinnamon, ginger, allspice, nutmeg, and cloves in a medium bowl.

Put the butter in the bowl of an electric mixer fitted with the paddle attachment and beat on medium-high speed until smooth. Add the brown sugar and continue beating until light and fluffy. Add the molasses and crystallized ginger, drop in the egg, and continue mixing until fully incorporated, stopping at least once to scrape the sides of the bowl. Reduce the mixing speed to low and gradually add the flour mixture, mixing just until the dough comes together. Scrape the dough into a large bowl, cover with plastic wrap, and set in the refrigerator to chill for at least 1 hour.

Position a rack in the middle of the oven and preheat the oven to 350ºF. Line baking sheets with parchment paper.

Shape the dough into balls about the size of slightly oversize golf balls. Roll the balls in granulated sugar and arrange them 2 to 3 inches apart on the prepared baking sheets. Bake for about 7 minutes, or until the cookies have spread, are light golden brown, and the cracks still appear moist.

Cool the cookies on the baking sheets set on wire racks for about 2 minutes before removing them to the racks to cool completely. Store the cookies in an airtight container or in a zip-top bag for up to 5 days.

One spring when visiting my sister and her family in Indiana, I took along a large bag of freshly made soft molasses cookies. My nephew Dillon was receiving his First Holy Communion that weekend, and I wanted to contribute something sweet to the four days our extended family would be celebrating together. No sooner had we arrived, however, than Dillon's younger brother, Logan, took command of the cookies. It seemed that every time I saw him, he was munching on another one. Within two days, the bag was filled with nothing but a few granules of sugar. I'm not sure whether anyone else had a chance to taste my molasses cookies that weekend, but I didn't mind. I must confess, the fact that he liked them so much and couldn't bring himself to share gave me great pleasure. Grown-ups and kids alike are sure to fall for these soft, mildly spiced molasses cookies. It's no wonder my nephew consumed the entire bag; the texture and flavor really are addictive. These cookies are designed to bake up soft. Just be sure, though, to watch them during the last couple of minutes of baking, and pull them from the oven when the cracks are still moist. You might be tempted to eat the whole batch, too.

Logan's Favorite Soft Molasses Cookies

MAKES ABOUT 35 COOKIES

2½ cups all-purpose flour
2 teaspoons baking soda
½ teaspoon salt
2 teaspoons ground ginger
1½ teaspoons ground cinnamon
¾ teaspoon ground cloves

½ cup vegetable shortening at room temperature
¼ cup (½ stick) unsalted butter at room temperature
1 cup packed light brown sugar
⅓ cup molasses
1 large egg
Granulated sugar for dipping

Whisk together the flour, baking soda, salt, ginger, cinnamon, and cloves in a medium bowl.

Put the shortening and butter in the bowl of an electric mixer fitted with the paddle attachment and beat on medium-high speed until smooth and thoroughly combined. Add the brown sugar and continue beating until light and fluffy. Pour in the molasses and beat until smooth. Drop in the egg and mix until combined, stopping at least once to scrape the sides of the bowl. Reduce the mixing speed to low and gradually add the flour mixture, mixing just until the dough comes together. Scrape the dough into a medium bowl, cover with plastic wrap, and set in the refrigerator to chill for at least 30 minutes to 1 hour.

Position a rack in the middle of the oven and preheat the oven to 350°F. Line baking sheets with parchment paper.

Shape the chilled dough into walnut-size balls, dip the tops in granulated sugar, and arrange them, sugar-side up, about 2 inches apart on the prepared baking sheets. (If your kitchen is quite warm and the dough balls become soft, set them in the refrigerator until chilled and fairly firm.) Bake for about 10 minutes, or until the cookies are puffed, light golden brown, and the cracks still appear moist.

Cool the cookies on the baking sheets set on wire racks for about 2 minutes before removing them to the racks to cool completely. Store the cookies in an airtight container or in a zip-top bag for up to 4 days.

Spicy gingerbread cutouts meet buttery shortbread in these cookies. At once crispy and tender, as well as intense with molasses and rich with butter, this shortbread is as homey and comforting as it is elegant and impressive. Making shortbread can be a tricky business. For the dough to be successful, it must contain just the right balance of butter, sugar, and flour. Too much butter, and the dough becomes slack and too soft to roll. Too much flour, and it is crumbly and dry and will refuse to come together. In addition, once cut, the cookies must remain chilled almost until the moment they hit the oven or they will become misshapen during baking. I think you will find that this recipe contains the right proportion of essential ingredients and bakes up nicely. A generous dose of spices and a spoonful of dark molasses impart just the right degree of gingerbread punch to the cookies. As with most shortbread, the final key is to bake the cookies at a low temperature for a longer time than you might expect. This method requires a bit of patience. However, it really does keep the cookies from spreading during baking and encourages them to develop just the right amount of crispness.

Gingerbread Shortbread Cookies

MAKES ABOUT 18 COOKIES

1³/4 cups all-purpose flour
¹/4 teaspoon salt
1¹/2 teaspoons ground ginger
1 teaspoon ground cinnamon
³/4 teaspoon ground cloves

¹/2 teaspoon freshly grated nutmeg
1 cup (2 sticks) unsalted butter at room temperature
³/4 cup sugar, plus more for sprinkling (optional)
1 tablespoon dark molasses

Whisk together the flour, salt, ginger, cinnamon, cloves, and nutmeg in a medium bowl.

Put the butter in the bowl of an electric mixer fitted with the paddle attachment and beat on medium-high speed until smooth. Add the ³/4 cup sugar and the molasses and continue beating until smooth. (Beating until light and fluffy isn't necessary here, as we want to incorporate as little air as possible into the dough.) Reduce the mixing speed to low and gradually add the flour mixture, mixing just until the dough comes together and forms moist clumps in the bowl. Turn the dough out onto a large piece of plastic wrap, shape into a disc, and wrap tightly. Set in the refrigerator to chill for at least 1 hour.

Position a rack in the middle of the oven and preheat the oven to 250°F. Line baking sheets with parchment paper.

Roll the chilled dough on a lightly floured work surface to about ¹/4 inch thick. Cut into 2³/4-inch rounds (or other desired shapes) and arrange the cookies about 1 inch apart on the prepared baking sheets. Set the cookies in the refrigerator until chilled again and firm, about 10 minutes.

Sprinkle with sugar (if desired) and bake for 40 to 45 minutes, or until the cookies are firm around the edges and chestnut brown in color.

Cool the cookies on the baking sheets set on wire racks for about 2 minutes before removing them to the racks to cool completely. Store the cookies in an airtight container or in a zip-top bag for up to 5 days.

Buttery, tender, and flirtatiously blond in color, old-fashioned shortbread represents the best of uncomplicated baking. Add a bit of ginger to the mix and this beloved treat transforms into an elegant gingerbread. Ground and crystallized gingers contribute a pleasing amount of heat and sweetness without being overwhelming. In addition, a small amount of rice flour (often used in Scottish shortbread and available in natural food stores and some supermarkets) contributes tenderness and just the right amount of crumbliness to the cookie. Sprinkled with a bit of turbinado sugar about halfway through the baking process, the shortbread has the ultimate appeal of being at once meltingly tender and slightly crunchy.

⇒ Twice-Gingered Shortbread ⇐

MAKES ONE 9-INCH SHORTBREAD, OR 16 WEDGES

$1^3/_4$ cups all-purpose flour
$1/_3$ cup rice flour
$1/_2$ teaspoon salt
$1/_2$ cup granulated sugar
1 teaspoon ground ginger

1 cup (2 sticks) cold unsalted butter, cut into about $1/_4$-inch pieces
$1/_4$ cup finely chopped crystallized ginger
3 tablespoons turbinado sugar or other raw or coarse-textured sugar

Position a rack in the middle of the oven and preheat the oven to 300°F. Butter a 9-by 3-inch springform pan. (A nonstick pan is helpful here.) Line the bottom with a round of parchment, and butter the parchment and sides of the pan again.

Combine the all-purpose flour, rice flour, salt, granulated sugar, and ground ginger in the bowl of an electric mixer fitted with the paddle attachment and begin mixing on medium-low speed. Toss in the butter pieces and continue mixing until the dough is crumbly, about 5 minutes. The butter pieces should be no bigger than the size of lentils. Add the crystallized ginger and mix until just incorporated.

Pour the crumbly dough into the prepared pan and spread evenly to the edges with your fingers. Press the dough firmly with the palm of your hand until the surface is smooth and even.

Set the filled pan on a baking sheet and bake the shortbread for about 25 minutes, or until barely golden brown. Remove it from the oven and, using a paring knife, carefully score the surface into 16 wedges. Using a wooden skewer, pierce the wedges, creating a decorative dot design, if desired. Sprinkle the top

evenly with the turbinado sugar, return the shortbread to the oven, and continue baking for about 20 minutes more, or until the shortbread is light golden brown.

Set the shortbread on a wire rack to cool in the pan for about 15 minutes. Remove the sides of the pan and cool completely before carefully sliding the shortbread off of the base of the pan.

When the shortbread is completely cooled, follow the score marks and cut into wedges. Store the shortbread in an airtight container, layered between sheets of parchment or waxed paper, for up to 1 week.

Traditional French madeleines receive a spicy update in this gingerbread version. Just as delicate and buttery as the originals, these madeleines acquire a hint of caramel-like sweetness from the addition of brown sugar, as well as a warm dose of spice from a combination of ground and crystallized gingers. Lemon zest and lemon extract also infuse them with a bright freshness that complements the gingery sweetness. Madeleines are really more like mini-sponge cakes than cookies. The mixing method reflects this, and there are a few things to keep in mind in order to ensure their light cakelike texture. First, it is important to whip the eggs and sugar to the ribbon stage. You'll know you have reached this point when the mixture has tripled in volume, lightened in color, and falls in thick ribbons from the whisk attachment. Whipping lots of air into the eggs and sugar will help the madeleines develop their cakey lightness. Next, the flour mixture and melted butter must be gently, but assuredly, folded into the egg mixture, again to ensure that they remain tender. Mixing or folding too enthusiastically will result in tough, flat madeleines. Finally, be sure to generously butter and flour your madeleine molds—even if you are using the nonstick version. Too often, I have taken great care with my batter, only to have the lovely cakes stick to poorly prepared pans. Unlike traditional madeleines, these gingerbread darlings remain moist for several days. To experience them at their best, however, try to consume them the day you bake them, or within a day or so. I hardly suspect you'll have trouble doing so.

→ Gingerbread Madeleines ←
MAKES 24 MADELEINES

3 large eggs
½ cup granulated sugar
2 tablespoons packed light brown sugar
1¼ cups cake flour
¼ teaspoon baking powder
¼ teaspoon salt

½ teaspoon ground ginger
½ cup (1 stick) unsalted butter, melted and cooled
⅛ teaspoon lemon extract or lemon oil
Grated zest of 1 lemon (about 1 tablespoon)
3 tablespoons finely chopped crystallized ginger
Confectioners' sugar for dusting

Position a rack in the middle of the oven and preheat the oven to 350°F. Generously butter and flour two 12-mold madeleine pans. (If you only have one pan, just wash it after baking the first batch of madeleines and then butter and flour it again. You will need to bake the next batch as soon as you remove the first batch from the pan, since the batter tends to deflate as it sits.)

Put the eggs in the bowl of an electric mixer fitted with the whisk attachment and begin whipping on medium-high speed to break up the yolks. Add the granulated and brown sugars, increase the mixing speed to high, and whip until the mixture is light yellow in color, tripled in volume, and forms thick ribbons when it falls from the whisk, about 5 minutes.

Meanwhile, whisk together the cake flour, baking powder, salt, and ground ginger in a medium bowl.

When the egg mixture is ready, remove the bowl from the mixer and, using a spatula, gradually fold in the flour mixture, folding just until you can no longer see flecks of flour. (Avoid being too aggressive here, as overenthusiastic folding will result in flat, tough madeleines.) Fold the melted butter into the batter, adding it in a slow, steady stream. (The butter will slightly deflate the batter, but that's okay.) Finally, fold in the lemon extract, lemon zest, and crystallized ginger.

Spoon the batter into the prepared pans, filling each mold about three-quarters full. Bake for about 10 minutes, or until the madeleines have spread, risen, and are light golden around the edges. (Avoid overbaking, as the madeleines will become too dry.)

Cool the madelines in the pans set on wire racks for about 3 minutes. Gently loosen them by pushing them toward the scalloped edges of the molds. Arrange the madeleines, smooth-sides down, on the rack to cool completely.

Serve the madeleines with a dusting of confectioners' sugar. Madeleines are best served the day they are baked, but they will store well in an airtight container, layered between sheets of parchment or waxed paper, for up to 3 days.

German *lebkuchen* is arguably one of the oldest forms of gingerbread. Related to ancient honey cakes first prepared in Egypt, Greece, and Rome, *lebkuchen* gained popularity in thirteenth-century German monasteries. The spice trade eventually provided a wider audience for this gingerbread, focusing particularly on the city of Nuremberg. As Eastern spices passed regularly through the city, bakers took advantage of combining them with honey (copiously produced in forests surrounding Nuremburg) to create the much-celebrated spice cake. *Lebkuchen* has been baked commercially in Nuremberg since at least the late fourteenth century. Today, only *lebkuchen* produced within the city proper can boast the name *Nürenberger Lebkuchen*. The following *lebkuchen* recipe is typical of the *braune* (brown) type, as it contains quite a lot of honey (traditionally the sweetener of choice), candied citrus peel, and an aromatic array of spices. These cookies maintain their shapes during baking while also remaining slightly soft. They store well, too. Their vibrant spiciness does mellow a bit over time, but they stay satisfyingly chewy. To ensure that they keep this consistency, store the *lebkuchen* in an airtight container along with a few apple slices for up to 2 days at a time. (Much longer and the fruit and cookies could get moldy.) Enjoy these *lebkuchen* plain, or, as they often are in Germany, coated with chocolate glaze. Either way, I think you will find them a flavorful departure from molasses-rich American gingerbread cookies.

Braune Lebkuchen

MAKES ABOUT TWENTY 3-INCH COOKIES

1/2 cup (1 stick) unsalted butter
3/4 cup honey
1/3 cup sugar
1 tablespoon finely chopped Candied Orange Peel (page 138) or store-bought candied orange peel
1 tablespoon finely chopped Candied Lemon Peel (page 138) or store-bought candied lemon peel
1 teaspoon grated lemon zest
1 teaspoon grated orange zest
2 1/2 cups all-purpose flour

3 tablespoons almond flour (almond meal)
3/4 teaspoon salt
1/2 teaspoon baking powder
1/4 teaspoon baking soda
2 teaspoons ground ginger
1 3/4 teaspoons ground cinnamon
1/2 teaspoon ground cloves
1/2 teaspoon ground aniseed

1 1/2 cups (1 recipe) Dark Chocolate Glaze (page 137; optional)

Combine the butter, honey, and sugar in a medium saucepan. Heat slowly over low heat, stirring occasionally, until the butter is melted and the sugar is dissolved. Remove from the heat, stir in the candied orange and lemon peels and the lemon and orange zests, and set aside until the mixture cools to room temperature, 45 minutes to 1 hour.

Position a rack in the middle of the oven and preheat the oven to 350°F. Line baking sheets with parchment paper.

Whisk together the all-purpose flour, almond flour, salt, baking powder, baking soda, ginger, cinnamon, cloves, and aniseed in a medium bowl.

Pour the cooled butter mixture into the bowl of an electric mixer fitted with the paddle attachment. Begin mixing on low speed and gradually incorporate the flour mixture, mixing just until the dough comes together. It will be smooth but a little sticky.

CONTINUED

Scrape the dough onto a work surface and knead several times into a smooth mass. (You shouldn't need to flour the work surface, but do so if necessary.) Roll the dough on a lightly floured work surface to 1/4 inch thick and cut into 3-inch rounds (or other desired shapes).

Arrange the cookies at least 1 1/2 inches apart on the prepared baking sheets. (Although not completely necessary, if you have space, set the sheets of cookies in the refrigerator to chill for about 10 minutes. This will help maintain their shapes even better in the oven.)

Bake for 12 to 15 minutes, or until the cookies are slightly puffed and light golden brown.

Cool the lebkuchen on the baking sheets set on wire racks for about 2 minutes before removing them to the racks to cool completely.

Coat the cooled lebkuchen with Dark Chocolate Glaze, if desired. Melt the glaze, if necessary, in a medium, wide-mouthed bowl until it is warm and smooth (see page 137). Gently drop the lebkuchen, one at a time, into the glaze, turning with a fork to coat completely. Using the fork, lift each cookie out of the glaze, tap gently on the edge of the bowl to allow any excess glaze to drip into the bowl, and set on a wire rack. Set the coated lebkuchen aside in a dry, cool area until the glaze is firm, about 1 hour. (If you don't use all of the glaze, reserve the remainder for later use, storing it as suggested on page 137.)

Serve the plain or coated lebkuchen immediately, or store them for at least several days, as they improve with age. To store the lebkuchen for more than a few days, put them in an airtight container, layered between sheets of parchment or waxed paper, for up to 1 month.

Opinions differ regarding the derivation of the word *lebkuchen*. Some allege that it comes from the Latin word *libum* (bread or sacrificial cake). Others suggest that the German *laib* (loaf) is related to, and became associated with, *leben* (life) due to the cake's nutritious qualities.

Braune (brown) *Lebkuchen* is one of the many subtypes of this spicy cookie, and even within this category there are many varieties. Simply put, *Braune Lebkuchen* refers to all *lebkuchen* that are cut into shapes and baked without thin, often rice flour, wafer bases. As with all types of *lebkuchen*, industry standards are strict for this variety, calling for each recipe to contain a certain percentage of sugar, flour, and nuts.

Literally translated as "pepper nuts" and sometimes referred to as *Pfefferkuchens* (pepper cakes), these German cookies are related to traditional *Lebkuchen*. To confuse things a bit further, *Pfeffernüsse* contain no pepper, but rather obtain their peppery character from a vibrant combination of spices, citrus, and sugar or honey. These cookies are traditionally quite hard and contain little or no fat. I admit, though, that I pull the cookies from the oven before they get too hard. The result is a cookie that is quite firm when baked, but that softens and mellows with age. You can actually keep the dough in the refrigerator for up to 2 weeks, or store the baked cookies for at least several days and up to 1 month before serving.

Pfeffernüsse

MAKES 74 COOKIES

3 large eggs
1 large egg yolk
1½ cups packed light brown sugar
3 cups all-purpose flour
¾ teaspoon salt
1 teaspoon baking powder
¼ teaspoon baking soda

1 tablespoon ground cinnamon
1 tablespoon ground ginger
¾ teaspoon ground cloves
½ teaspoon ground allspice
2 teaspoons grated orange zest
Confectioners' sugar for rolling (optional)

Put the eggs and egg yolk in the bowl of an electric mixer fitted with the whisk attachment and begin whipping on high speed to break up the yolks. Reduce the mixing speed to medium-low and add the brown sugar. Increase the mixing speed to high once again and whip until the mixture is light yellow in color, tripled in volume, and forms thick ribbons when it falls from the whisk, about 5 minutes.

Meanwhile, whisk together the flour, salt, baking powder, baking soda, cinnamon, ginger, cloves, allspice, and orange zest in a medium bowl.

Remove the whisk attachment from the electric mixer and replace it with the paddle attachment. Beat the whipped eggs on low speed and gradually add the flour mixture, beating just until the dough comes together. (It will be slightly crumbly, but smooth and easy to handle.) Scrape the dough into a medium bowl, cover with plastic wrap, and set in the refrigerator to chill for at least 3 hours or overnight.

Position a rack in the middle of the oven and preheat the oven to 325°F. Line baking sheets with parchment paper.

Roll small scoops (about 2 teaspoons) of dough into balls and arrange them about 1 inch apart on the prepared baking sheets. Bake for about 10 minutes, or until the Pfeffernüsse are firm and light golden brown.

Cool the Pfeffernüsse on the baking sheets set on wire racks for about 2 minutes before removing them to the racks to cool completely. Roll in confectioners' sugar, if desired, and serve immediately, or store them for at least several days, as they improve with age. To store the Pfeffernüsse for more than a few days, with or without the sugar coating, put them in an airtight container or in a zip-top bag for up to 1 month.

My sister Erica not only loves to eat biscotti, but she is a whiz at making them. Always keen to try another biscotti recipe, Erica approaches each one with a particular bent. She likes them soft. According to my sister, hard biscotti should be relegated to those who enjoy risking scraped gums while eating, or who like to dunk their unyielding cookies in *vin santo* or coffee. These gingerbread biscotti are delicately spiced, not too sweet, and soft inside while ever so slightly crisp on the outside. A mixture of ginger, cinnamon, and sugar sprinkled on the cookies before and during baking adds extra flavor and texture to these golden lovelies, as well. I think my discerning sister would approve.

→ Soft Gingerbread Biscotti ←

MAKES 30 BISCOTTI

2³/₄ cups all-purpose flour
2 teaspoons baking powder
¼ teaspoon salt
3 teaspoons ground ginger
3 teaspoons ground cinnamon
½ teaspoon ground cloves

³/₄ cup plus 3 tablespoons granulated sugar
¼ cup packed light brown sugar
3 large eggs
2 tablespoons unsalted butter, melted and cooled
1½ teaspoons vanilla extract
1 large egg white, lightly beaten

Position a rack in the middle of the oven and preheat the oven to 350°F. Line a large baking sheet with parchment paper.

Whisk together the flour, baking powder, salt, 2 teaspoons of the ginger, 2 teaspoons of the cinnamon, the cloves, the ³/₄ cup granulated sugar, and the brown sugar in a large bowl.

Whisk together the eggs, butter, and vanilla extract in a medium bowl. Pour the egg mixture into the flour mixture, stirring with a wooden spoon until the dough comes together in a soft and slightly sticky mass.

Turn the dough out onto a lightly floured work surface and knead several times until smooth. Divide the dough in half and shape each piece into a log about 8 inches long and 2 inches wide. Set the logs about 3 inches apart on the prepared baking sheet.

Stir together the remaining 1 teaspoon of ginger, 1 teaspoon of cinnamon, and 3 tablespoons of granulated sugar in a small bowl. Brush the logs with the egg white and sprinkle with about one-third of the spiced sugar mixture.

Bake the logs for 25 to 30 minutes, or until they are puffed and golden brown. Cool the logs on the baking sheets set on wire racks for about 10 minutes.

Reduce the oven temperature to 300°F.

Using a serrated knife and cutting on the diagonal, cut each log into about fifteen ½-inch-thick slices. Arrange the biscotti, flat-side down, on the baking sheet and sprinkle with another one-third of the sugar mixture. Bake for about 6 minutes, or until the biscotti are light golden brown. Turn the biscotti, sprinkle with the remaining sugar mixture, and bake for about 6 minutes more.

Cool the biscotti on the baking sheet set on a wire rack for about 5 minutes before removing them to the rack to cool completely. Store the biscotti in an airtight container or in a zip-top bag for up to 4 days.

My youngest sister, Alexis, is often my partner in the kitchen. She eagerly takes on important tasks like assembling and storing ingredients, wiping down the countertops, and drying dishes. Her biggest job, though, is the one for which she is always prepared and enthusiastic: taste testing! Before the empty bowls of batter or used spatulas go into the sink, Alexis happily takes them on, spoon at the ready. We both agree it makes cleanup easier, after all. Of course, she helps me taste the baked goodies, too, and always gives her honest opinion. When I cut a small square of these freshly baked gingerbread blondies for Alexis, the first thing she said was, "Oh, wow." After that, I decided I couldn't possibly call this recipe anything else. I was pleased that many others who tried these blondies echoed Alexis's response. Although modest in appearance, they are alluring, nonetheless. Lightly cracked on top and chestnut brown in color, they are just on the brink of gooey in the center when they come out of the oven. Once cooled, the blondies cut easily into super-moist squares that are gently spiced and rich with caramel and butterscotch flavors. Hopefully, they will inspire you, too, to the level of "wow."

Alexis's "Oh, Wow" Gingerbread Blondies

MAKES ONE 9-INCH PAN

2³/₄ cups all-purpose flour
1 teaspoon salt
³/₄ teaspoon baking soda
³/₄ teaspoon baking powder
2 teaspoons ground ginger
2 teaspoons ground cinnamon
1 cup (2 sticks) unsalted butter, melted and cooled

1 cup packed dark brown sugar
³/₄ cup molasses
1 teaspoon vanilla extract
1 large egg
2 tablespoons heavy (whipping) cream
Confectioners' sugar for dusting (optional)

Position a rack in the middle of the oven and preheat the oven to 350°F. Butter and flour a 9-by-2-inch square baking pan.

Whisk together the flour, salt, baking soda, baking powder, ginger, and cinnamon in a medium bowl.

Whisk together the butter, brown sugar, molasses, and vanilla extract in a large bowl. Drop in the egg and pour in the cream, whisking until incorporated. Using a wooden spoon, gradually stir in the flour mixture, mixing until smooth.

Pour the batter into the prepared pan. Bake for 20 to 25 minutes, or until the blondies are chestnut brown in color, puffed,

slightly cracked on top, and a skewer inserted in the center comes out with a few soft or gooey crumbs.

Set the blondies on a wire rack to cool completely in the pan.

Serve the blondies cut into squares and dusted with confectioners' sugar, if desired. Store the blondies in an airtight container, layered between sheets of parchment or waxed paper, for up to 4 days.

My best friend, Kate, loves to cook and experiment in the kitchen. When it comes to dessert, however, she often turns to her mother's favorite brownie recipe. Mrs. Reed was quite an accomplished cook and hostess, albeit one with an Achilles' heel—she never had much success with baking. Mrs. Reed did find salvation with these brownies, however, and Kate recalls that she frequently turned to this recipe. It came as no surprise to me that my stylish friend and her equally elegant mother attribute their favorite brownie recipe to none other than the inimitable Katharine Hepburn. Whether Miss Hepburn ever baked these brownies, Kate (who ironically shares the name) and I don't know. The famed actress apparently loved chocolate and is alleged to have eaten it every day, so I assume she enjoyed brownies, too. Regardless of the story's veracity, this recipe has become the basis for my gingerbread version. I have enhanced these brownies in several ways. First, I have added warm spices and dark brown sugar to inspire their new gingerbread role. Next, I have added more chocolate, which is chopped and added to the batter before baking. Finally, I have decreased the baking time to ensure that the brownies remain really moist. If you prefer your brownies to be a bit more cakelike, watch the clock and leave them in the oven for about 5 to 10 minutes longer than I suggest.

→ Kate's Gingerbread Brownies ←
MAKES ONE 8-INCH PAN

- 3 tablespoons all-purpose flour
- 1 tablespoon Dutch-process cocoa powder
- 1/4 teaspoon salt
- 1 1/2 teaspoons ground ginger
- 1 1/2 teaspoons ground cinnamon
- 1/4 teaspoon ground cloves
- 1/8 teaspoon ground cardamom
- 1/2 cup (1 stick) unsalted butter at room temperature

- 2 ounces unsweetened chocolate, chopped
- 3/4 cup granulated sugar
- 1/4 cup packed dark brown sugar
- 1/2 teaspoon vanilla extract
- 2 large eggs
- 2 1/2 ounces bittersweet or semisweet chocolate, chopped
- 1/4 cup chopped crystallized ginger
- Confectioners' sugar for dusting (optional)

Position a rack in the middle of the oven and preheat the oven to 325°F. Butter and flour an 8-inch square baking pan.

Whisk together the flour, cocoa powder, salt, ginger, cinnamon, cloves, and cardamom in a medium bowl.

Combine the butter and the unsweetened chocolate in a medium, heatproof bowl. Set the bowl over a saucepan filled with about 1 1/2 inches of simmering water (being sure not to let the bottom of the bowl touch the water) and stir occasionally until the chocolate and butter have melted and the mixture is smooth. Remove the bowl from the saucepan and set aside to cool slightly, about 10 minutes. (You can also melt the mixture in the microwave, heating it at about 20-second intervals and stirring periodically until it is melted and smooth.)

Using a wooden spoon or heatproof spatula, stir the granulated and brown sugars into the melted chocolate and butter mixture. Add the vanilla extract and drop in the eggs, one at a time, mixing until smooth. Sprinkle in the flour mixture, again mixing until smooth. Fold in the chopped bittersweet chocolate and crystallized ginger.

Pour the batter into the prepared pan. Bake for 25 to 30 minutes, or until the brownies are just barely set and a wooden skewer inserted in the center comes out with a few sticky crumbs.

Set the brownies on a wire rack to cool completely in the pan.

Serve the brownies cut into squares and dusted with confectioners' sugar, if desired. Store the brownies in an airtight container, layered between sheets of parchment or waxed paper, for up to 4 days.

One of the best things about gingerbread is that, in addition to being delicious in its pure form, it also combines obligingly with other yummy ingredients, transforming into new and tempting desserts. Fresh or leftover gingerbread works beautifully here. Cast these cakes and cookies as the stars of a dish, or use them in supporting sweet and spicy roles to complement creamy, custardy, fruity, or chocolaty ingredients. Gingerbread in virtually every form freezes well, too. Even when you don't feel like starting completely from scratch, you can still enjoy a gingerbread dessert anytime.

CHAPTER THREE: Desserts

Every dessert in this chapter takes its cue from a more familiar and traditional dish. Again, this is what makes gingerbread so great. Although it has its own unique character, gingerbread is enhanced by a wide variety of ingredients. Some of these desserts are homey and comforting, while others are refined and elegant. A few are suited to fall and winter, and still others would be just right for spring and summer. Whether you are in the mood for a toffee pudding, an ice cream sandwich, or a *bûche de Noël*, you will find a delicious diversity of flavors and textures here. All of these desserts pay tribute to old-fashioned gingerbread, though, and the traditional, spicy sweetness that seduced us to fall for it in the first place.

This bread pudding is my ode to autumn in Burgundy. It was there during a trip in October that I first experienced the region's famous *pain d'épices* (spice bread) and where I fell in love with quince. For nearly a week, renowned cookbook author and teacher Anne Willan hosted us at her Château du Feÿ. We were there to write, cook, and eat, and Anne graciously assisted in our endeavors. She gave us free rein not only of one of her kitchens, but of her enormous seventeenth-century garden, as well. The quince trees were fragrant with abundant fruit that season. Clustered among rows of pumpkins and Swiss chard, they appeared strong and stoic, their branches struggling to remain outstretched, burdened as they were with the weight of their successful offspring. Happily for us, the chef offered some relief to the little trees and prepared a gorgeous quince tarte Tatin. The glistening, amber-colored caramel and perfumed fruit were intoxicating. Loath to blaspheme the traditional apple version, many of us, nonetheless, whispered that we preferred the quince tarte. I was smitten with this yellow-skinned, rock-hard fruit and how it transformed during cooking. As the quince simmered in butter and sugar, the unyielding white flesh gradually relinquished to the heat and emerged as a delicate, pearlike sweetmeat. Seduced by this metamorphosis, I wasted no time gathering more fruit from the trees' generous branches. My friend Joan and I peeled and chopped a basketful of quince, tossed them into one of Anne's gleaming copper pots, and covered them with sugar syrup. We set the pot over a low flame and then made ourselves comfortable by the stove, chatting and occasionally acknowledging the barely bubbling fruit with a gentle stir, until we finally coaxed them into preserves. Fortunately, fresh quince and the quince jelly called for in this dessert are readily available in the United States. Whether you cook the jelly yourself or buy it in a jar, I hope you will make this pudding. Soft and creamy, not too sweet, and fragrant with spices and orange, this bread pudding is comforting enough to enjoy on a cold evening in front of the fire, and elegant enough to serve at a dinner party. A drizzle of crème anglaise, if you choose to use it, provides a lovely final (and, dare I say, French) flourish.

Burgundian Bread & Butter Pudding
WITH PAIN D'ÉPICES & QUINCE

MAKES ONE 9-INCH LAYER CAKE

2 cups whole milk

1 cup heavy (whipping) cream

3 large eggs

2 large egg yolks

1/4 cup granulated sugar

1/4 cup packed dark brown sugar

1/4 cup honey

1 teaspoon ground ginger

1 teaspoon ground cinnamon

1/4 teaspoon ground aniseed

1/4 teaspoon freshly grated nutmeg

1/4 teaspoon salt

1 teaspoon grated orange zest

1 loaf (1/2 recipe) day-old Pain d'Épices (page 115)

5 tablespoons unsalted butter at room temperature

1/3 cup quince jelly

Crème Anglaise (page 133) for drizzling (optional)

CONTINUED

Position a rack in the middle of the oven and preheat the oven to 325°F. Butter a 9-by-2-inch square baking pan.

Whisk together the milk, cream, eggs, egg yolks, granulated and brown sugars, honey, ginger, cinnamon, aniseed, nutmeg, salt, and orange zest in a large bowl.

Using a serrated knife, cut the pain d'épices into 16 slices about 1/4 to 3/8 inch thick. (You'll use about three-quarters of the loaf.) Butter the slices on one side. Spread the jelly on 8 of the slices and press the pieces together to make 8 sandwiches. Cut the sandwiches on the diagonal, creating 16 triangles. Shingle the triangles in 2 rows in the prepared pan, leaning one against the other in a crisscrossed manner. Pour the milk and egg mixture over the top, coating the sandwiches completely and pressing them gently into the custard. Set aside to soak for about 10 minutes.

Cover the pan loosely with buttered aluminum foil, set on a baking sheet, and bake for 25 minutes. Remove the foil and continue baking for about 35 minutes more, or until the custard and bread are puffed and golden brown.

Set the pudding on a wire rack to cool in the pan for about 15 minutes, if serving it warm, or cool completely and serve at room temperature or cold.

Serve the pudding cut into squares and drizzled with Crème Anglaise, if desired.

If you like gingerbread and enjoy bread pudding, this dish is for you. Like most bread puddings, it comes together quickly and easily and, what's more, makes use of leftover gingerbread cake. Because even stale or day-old gingerbread remains somewhat moist, this pudding takes on a uniquely luscious texture. The gingerbread slices transform into soft, creamy pillows as they bake in the delicately spiced custard, while the bits poking out of the velvety pool develop into pleasingly crisp morsels. This pudding really has no need for an accompaniment, but if you wish, a dollop of whipped cream would do nicely.

Gingerbread Bread Pudding

MAKES ONE 1½-QUART DISH OF PUDDING

1 pound day-old gingerbread cake, cut into ¼-inch-thick square slices
4 large eggs
1½ cups whole milk
½ cup heavy (whipping) cream
½ cup granulated sugar
¼ cup packed dark brown sugar

1 teaspoon ground cinnamon
½ teaspoon ground ginger
Pinch of salt
1 teaspoon vanilla extract

Whipped Cream (page 132) for serving (optional)

Preheat the oven to 350°F. Butter a 1½-quart rectangular or oval baking dish.

Shingle the gingerbread slices in the prepared dish (I usually form two rows down the length of the dish). Whisk together the remaining ingredients (except the Whipped Cream) in a large bowl to make the custard. Pour the mixture over the gingerbread, gently pressing the pieces into the custard, and set aside for about 10 minutes.

Set the bread pudding on a baking sheet and bake for 30 to 35 minutes, or until it is puffed and golden.

Serve spoonfuls of the pudding hot, at room temperature, or cold with the Whipped Cream, if desired.

Some time ago, I developed an obsession for English sticky toffee pudding. I gathered recipes, researched shops in England where I could order it, and finally decided to develop a gingerbread version. I'm sure this was hardly a novel idea, but if I do say so myself, it certainly was a good one. The pudding in its traditional form—a combination of dense, date-flavored cake and toffee-like sauce—takes beautifully to the addition of spices and molasses. The result is a sweet and spicy gingerbread pudding soaked with a sticky, buttery, brown sugary sauce. You might think an 8-inch pudding is rather mean, but a small wedge of this sticky decadence will certainly satisfy your toffee craving. Well, if you must, serve it with a small dollop of whipped cream.

Sticky Toffee Gingerbread Pudding

MAKES ONE 8-INCH PUDDING

CAKE

1¼ cups lightly packed pitted dates, finely chopped
¾ cup water
¼ cup brewed espresso or strong coffee
1 teaspoon Dutch-process cocoa powder
1 cup all-purpose flour
1½ teaspoons baking powder
½ teaspoon salt
1 teaspoon ground ginger
1 teaspoon ground cinnamon
½ teaspoon ground cloves
¼ teaspoon freshly grated nutmeg

½ cup (1 stick) unsalted butter at room temperature
5 tablespoons molasses
2 tablespoons heavy (whipping) cream
1 large egg

SYRUP

1 cup packed light brown sugar
½ cup (1 stick) unsalted butter at room temperature
¼ cup water
¼ teaspoon salt

Whipped Cream (page 132) for serving (optional)

Position a rack in the middle of the oven and preheat the oven to 350° F. Butter and flour an 8-by-2-inch round cake pan.

TO MAKE THE CAKE

Combine the dates, water, espresso, and cocoa powder in a small saucepan. Bring to a boil over medium-high heat, stirring occasionally. Reduce the heat to low and simmer for about 5 minutes, or until the dates are tender and the mixture has thickened. Remove from the heat and set aside.

Whisk together the flour, baking powder, salt, ginger, cinnamon, cloves, and nutmeg in a large bowl.

Put the butter in the bowl of an electric mixer fitted with the paddle attachment and beat on medium-high speed until smooth. Pour in the molasses and beat until incorporated. Add the cream, drop in the egg, and beat for about 2 minutes, stopping at least once to scrape the sides of the bowl. The batter might appear curdled at this point, but not to worry. Reduce the mixing speed to medium-low and gradually incorporate the flour mixture, stopping once or twice to scrape the sides of the bowl. Add the date mixture and mix just until combined.

Pour the batter into the prepared pan and bake for about 25 minutes, or until the top is lightly cracked and a wooden skewer inserted in the center comes out clean (some sticky crumbs are okay, too).

Combine the brown sugar, butter, water, and salt in a small saucepan. Cook over medium-low heat, stirring occasionally, until the butter and sugar are melted and the mixture is smooth. Simmer, stirring occasionally, for about 6 minutes, or until the syrup is slightly reduced and thickened to a loose honey consistency. Remove from the heat and set aside, keeping warm.

Remove the cake from the oven and set on a wire rack. While the cake is still hot, poke holes all over the top, using a toothpick or wooden skewer. Spoon about half of the warm syrup over the cake and set aside to cool in the pan for about 25 minutes.

Run a paring knife around the edges of the soaked cake to loosen them a bit and invert the cake onto a serving plate. (If possible, it's helpful to have a plate with a large enough rim so the sauce doesn't flow over the sides.) Poke holes again all over the top, spoon the rest of the syrup over the top, and set the cake aside to soak for at least 10 more minutes.

Serve the warm pudding cut into wedges and drizzle with any excess syrup that has dripped down the sides. Spoon a dollop of the Whipped Cream on top of each wedge, if desired.

Born in Chattanooga, Tennessee, in the early twentieth century, the Moon Pie takes on new life in this gingerbread incarnation. The traditional chocolate-covered cookie-and-marshmallow sandwich becomes hardly more serious but definitely spicier here. Whole-wheat flour lends satisfying nuttiness to the graham crackers, while the ginger, cinnamon, and nutmeg provide warmth and subtle spiciness. Molasses-maple marshmallows complement the flavor and texture of the crackers, providing them with a soft, cushy center. Finally, the dark chocolate glaze cloaks the pies in mahogany sweetness. Best of all, the glaze remains firm once it dries so it won't melt in your hands and cramp your sophisticated Moon Pie-eating style.

→ Gingerbread-Maple Moon Pies ←
MAKES 18 MOON PIES

GINGERBREAD GRAHAM CRACKERS

1½ cups all-purpose flour
1 cup whole-wheat flour
¾ cup packed light brown sugar
1 teaspoon baking soda
1 teaspoon salt
¾ teaspoon ground ginger
½ teaspoon ground cinnamon
¼ teaspoon freshly grated nutmeg

½ cup (1 stick) cold unsalted butter, cut into pieces
¼ cup honey
¼ cup molasses
¼ cup whole milk
2 teaspoons vanilla extract

Molasses-Maple Marshmallows (recipe follows)

1½ cups (1 recipe) Dark Chocolate Glaze (page 137)

TO MAKE THE GINGERBREAD GRAHAM CRACKERS

Combine the all-purpose flour, whole-wheat flour, brown sugar, baking soda, salt, ginger, cinnamon, and nutmeg in the bowl of an electric mixer fitted with the paddle attachment and begin mixing on medium-low speed. Add the butter, about 1 tablespoon at a time, increase the mixing speed to medium, and continue beating until the mixture resembles the texture of fine bread crumbs. Whisk together the honey, molasses, milk, and vanilla extract in a small bowl. Pour the honey mixture into the beating crumbs, mixing just until the dough comes together.

Turn the dough out onto a large sheet of plastic wrap, press into a large disc, and wrap tightly. Set the dough in the refrigerator to chill for about 2 hours.

Position a rack in the middle of the oven and preheat the oven to 350°F. Line baking sheets with parchment paper.

Roll the chilled dough on a lightly floured work surface to about ⅛ inch thick. Cut into 2¾-inch discs and arrange about 1 inch apart on the prepared baking sheets. Using a fork, dock the graham crackers (poke them with holes). Bake for 12 to 15 minutes, or until the crackers are golden brown and firm.

Cool the crackers on the baking sheets set on wire racks for about 2 minutes before removing them to the racks to cool completely. The crackers can be stored at this point in an airtight container or in a zip-top bag for up to 4 days.

Set a large wire rack over a baking sheet or sheet of aluminum foil. Arrange half of the graham crackers, top-sides down, on the rack. Spoon about 1 heaping tablespoon of marshmallow on each cracker. Top with the remaining graham crackers, pressing gently to spread the marshmallow just about to the edges. Set aside until the marshmallow is firm, about 2 hours.

Melt the glaze, if necessary, in a medium, wide-mouthed bowl until it is warm and smooth. Gently drop the Moon Pies, one at a time, into the glaze, turning with a fork to coat them completely. Using the fork, lift each pie out of the glaze, tap gently on the edge of the bowl to allow any excess glaze to drip down the sides of the pie, and return it to the wire rack. Set the coated pies aside in a dry, cool area until the glaze is firm, about 1 hour. (If you don't use all of the glaze, reserve the remainder for later use.)

Serve the Moon Pies whole or cut in half to reveal their pretty layers. Store the Moon Pies in an airtight container, layered between sheets of parchment or waxed paper, for up to 1 week.

MOLASSES-MAPLE

Marshmallows

- 1/2 cup granulated sugar
- 2 tablespoons packed dark brown sugar
- 5 tablespoons water
- 2 tablespoons light corn syrup
- 1 tablespoon molasses
- 2 teaspoons unflavored gelatin
- 2 large egg whites
- 1 teaspoon vanilla extract
- 1/8 teaspoon maple extract

Combine the granulated sugar, brown sugar, 3 tablespoons of the water, the corn syrup, and molasses in a medium saucepan. Cook over medium heat, stirring occasionally, until the sugars are melted and the mixture is smooth. Bring to a boil, place a candy thermometer in the mixture, and continue to cook, without stirring, to 238°F (soft-ball stage), 7 to 10 minutes.

Meanwhile, pour the remaining 2 tablespoons of water into a small bowl, sprinkle the gelatin on top, and set aside to soften (bloom), about 5 minutes. Put the egg whites in the bowl of an electric mixer fitted with the whisk attachment. (Because this is such a small amount of egg whites, you can also use a handheld mixer.) Whip on medium-high speed to soft peaks. Ideally, you want the meringue and boiling sugar to be ready at the same time. If the meringue is ready before the sugar, reduce the mixing speed to low while continuing to cook the sugar.

As soon as the sugar reaches the desired temperature, remove the saucepan from the heat and stir in the softened gelatin. Reduce the mixing speed to medium-low and gradually incorporate the hot sugar into the whipping egg whites, allowing it to drizzle in a steady, thin stream down the side of the bowl. This will prevent the sugar from forming hard strands around the interior of the bowl. As soon as all of the sugar is incorporated, add the vanilla and maple extracts, increase the mixing speed to high, and whip until the marshmallow is thick and the bowl is cool to the touch.

Immediately fill the Moon Pies as instructed. (Alternatively, make individual marshmallows to serve with hot cocoa or enjoy as confections. Line an 8 1/2-by-4 1/4-by-3-inch loaf pan with parchment paper and brush lightly with vegetable oil. Evenly spread the marshmallow mixture in the pan, set aside for at least 6 hours or overnight, and cut into squares. Store in an airtight container, separated between sheets of parchment or waxed paper, for up to 1 week.)

These ice cream sandwiches take the time-honored dessert to a new level. I can't think of a happier pair than spicy, chewy ginger cookies and creamy pumpkin ice cream. Happily, the cookies remain soft even when frozen. As a result, when you bite into the sandwich, the ice cream stays put and doesn't squirt out all over the place. Even on a cool autumn day, these frozen treats will warm your heart and comfort your taste buds.

Gingerbread-Pumpkin Ice Cream Sandwiches

MAKES 8 SANDWICHES

1 cup Pumpkin-Gingersnap Ice Cream (page 94), gingersnaps omitted and slightly softened

16 Giant Chewy Ginger Cookies (page 52)

Spoon about 2 tablespoons of ice cream on the underside of a ginger cookie. Place another cookie on top, bottom-side down, pressing gently, and wrap in plastic wrap. Set in the freezer and prepare the remaining sandwiches. Freeze until firm, about 1 hour.

Serve the sandwiches directly from the freezer, or let them sit for a minute or two to soften slightly.

When it comes to impressive, beautiful desserts, few can compare with trifle. Layered colorfully in a large glass bowl, the combination of jammy fruit, cake, custard, and whipped cream is sure to entice even the most disciplined dieter. Although this version makes use of prepared gingerbread cake, the addition of blackberries makes it is as good a choice for spring or summer as it is for fall or winter. It might not seem an obvious pairing, but the sweet-tartness of the blackberries marries well with the spicy, molasses-imbued gingerbread. To woo you further, I suggest using frozen berries (fresh are fine, of course, if they're in season), so you really can prepare this dessert any time of year.

→ Gingerbread-Blackberry Trifle ←

MAKES ONE 3- TO 4 -QUART BOWL OF TRIFLE

BLACKBERRY SAUCE

Two 10-ounce bags frozen blackberries, slightly thawed, or 5 cups fresh blackberries, plus fresh black-berries for garnish (optional)

1 cup sugar
   Grated zest and juice of $1/2$ lemon

$1^1/2$ to 2 pounds day-old gingerbread cake

2 cups (1 recipe) cold Crème Anglaise (page 133)

4 cups (1 recipe) Whipped Cream (page 132)

   Confectioners' sugar for garnish (optional)

TO MAKE THE BLACKBERRY SAUCE

Stir together the blackberries, sugar, and lemon zest in a medium saucepan. Cook over medium-low heat, stirring occasionally and mashing the berries slightly, for about 20 minutes, or until the mixture is reduced by about one-quarter and syrupy. Stir in the lemon juice, pour the berries into a shallow dish or bowl, and set aside to cool to room temperature.

Cut the gingerbread into about 2- or 3-inch squares. Dip the gingerbread into the cooled blackberry sauce, coating on all sides. Place the squares in the bottom of a 3- to 4-quart trifle bowl, pressing together gently. Spread any remaining blackberry sauce evenly over the coated gingerbread. Pour the Crème Anglaise over the gingerbread and spoon dollops of the Whipped Cream over the top. Set the trifle in the refrigerator to chill for at least 30 minutes.

Drop some fresh blackberries over the top of the trifle and dust with confectioners' sugar, if desired. Serve generous spoonfuls of chilled trifle in dessert bowls.

My husband, Chris, is crazy about tortes. He loves nearly any dessert that involves multiple layers of cake or crust, cream, and fruit. One year, I perfected a blueberry-cream cheese torte, which elicited great raves from my beloved taste tester and self-proclaimed dessert aficionado. Then it got me thinking, What could I do with gingerbread? One evening in the kitchen was all it took. A spicy gingersnap cookie crust, delicately sweet cream cheese filling, and thick topping of pumpkin butter resulted in a snuggly layered trio of creamy, crunchy lusciousness. This dessert will make quite an impression at the table, but it is really a snap to put together. The crust can be prepared with leftover (even stale) homemade or store-bought gingersnaps, and the cream cheese filling takes seconds, literally, to whip together. The pumpkin butter requires a bit more time at the stove and somewhat of a watchful eye. It is so superb, though, that in addition to using it in this recipe, I suggest you cook up some extra and seal it in jars. This butter takes toast to a new level and adds delicious squashy intensity to slices of Pain d'Épices (page 115), as well. Some days, however, call for just the jar of pumpkin butter and a big spoon.

Chris's Pumpkin-Gingerbread Torte

MAKES ONE 8-INCH TORTE

PUMPKIN BUTTER

- 2 cups pumpkin purée
- 1 cup granulated sugar
- $1/2$ cup packed light brown sugar
- $1/4$ teaspoon salt
- 1 teaspoon ground cinnamon
- 1 teaspoon ground ginger
- $1/4$ teaspoon ground allspice
- $1/4$ teaspoon freshly grated nutmeg
- 1 teaspoon vanilla extract

CRUST

- $1^1/2$ cups (about 20 cookies) finely ground Old-Time Gingersnaps (page 39) or store-bought gingersnaps
- 6 tablespoons unsalted butter, melted

CREAM CHEESE FILLING

One 8-ounce package cream cheese at room temperature
- $3/4$ cup confectioners' sugar
- $1/3$ cup heavy (whipping) cream
- 1 teaspoon vanilla extract

TO MAKE THE PUMPKIN BUTTER

Stir together the pumpkin purée, granulated and brown sugars, salt, cinnamon, ginger, allspice, and nutmeg in a medium, heavy-bottomed saucepan. Cook over medium-low heat for about 10 minutes, stirring occasionally. Reduce the heat to low and cook, stirring frequently, for 40 to 50 minutes, or until the butter is dark amber in color, caramelized, and reduced by about half. Remove the butter to a bowl, stir in the vanilla extract, and set aside to cool completely.

TO MAKE THE CRUST

Position a rack in the middle of the oven and preheat the oven to 325ºF. Butter an 8-by-2-inch springform pan. (A nonstick pan is quite helpful here.)

Stir together the ground gingersnaps and butter in a medium bowl until moist. Using your fingers, spread the buttered crumbs evenly over the bottom of the prepared pan, pressing firmly and creating about a $1/4$- to $1/3$-inch rim up the sides. Bake for 8 to 10 minutes, or until the crust is fragrant and set. Remove to a wire rack to cool completely.

Put the cream cheese in the bowl of an electric mixer fitted with the paddle attachment and beat on medium speed until smooth. Reduce the mixing speed to low and add the confectioners' sugar. Increase the mixing speed to medium again and beat until smooth. Pour in the cream and vanilla extract and continue beating until smooth.

Spoon the cream cheese filling on top of the cooled crust, spreading evenly. Set in the refrigerator to chill for at least 45 minutes.

Spread the pumpkin butter evenly over the cream cheese layer. Return the torte to the refrigerator to chill for at least 30 minutes or overnight.

Carefully remove the sides of the springform pan and slide the torte off of the bottom of the pan and onto a serving plate. Serve the torte cut into wedges.

I have always loved the idea of preparing a *bûche de Noël* (Yule log) at Christmas. Admittedly more time-consuming than a pan of brownies, the *bûche* is as much a showpiece as it is a delicious addition to the dessert table. In reality, though, this *petite bûche* is perfect for a small gathering and requires about as much time as an iced layer cake. You could even assemble it one day and prepare the mushroom decorations the next. However you decide to organize the task, the end result is worth a bit of time in the kitchen.

Gingerbread Bûche de Noël WITH CHOCOLATE & CHESTNUT BUTTERCREAMS

MAKES ONE 7-INCH-LONG CAKE (APPROXIMATE SIZE)

1/2 cup cake flour
3 tablespoons almond flour (almond meal)
1/4 teaspoon salt
1/8 teaspoon baking soda
1 1/2 teaspoons ground ginger
1 1/2 teaspoons ground cinnamon
3/4 teaspoon ground cloves
1/2 teaspoon freshly grated nutmeg
4 large eggs, separated
1/4 cup packed light brown sugar
1 tablespoon dark molasses

1 1/2 teaspoons vanilla extract
5 tablespoons granulated sugar

Confectioners' sugar for dusting
Chestnut Buttercream (page 84) for filling
Chocolate Buttercream (page 84) for icing
Meringue Mushrooms (page 85) for garnish
Chopped pistachios for garnish

Position a rack in the middle of the oven and preheat the oven to 350°F. Butter a 15 1/2-by-10 1/2-by-1-inch baking sheet. Line the bottom with parchment paper, butter the parchment, and dust the baking sheet with flour.

Whisk together the cake flour, almond flour, salt, baking soda, ginger, cinnamon, cloves, and nutmeg in a medium bowl.

Put the egg yolks in the bowl of an electric mixer fitted with the whisk attachment and begin whipping on medium-high speed. Add the brown sugar and molasses and continue whipping until lightened in color and thickened to a thick pudding consistency. Remove the mixture to a large bowl and stir in the vanilla extract.

Wash the mixing bowl and whisk attachment thoroughly, return them to the mixer, and put the egg whites in the bowl. Whip on

high speed until the whites are frothy. Gradually incorporate the granulated sugar and whip to soft peaks.

Fold about 1 cup of the egg whites into the egg yolk mixture. Gradually add the flour mixture, folding until just incorporated. Fold in the remaining egg whites, about one-quarter at a time, until the batter is smooth and light. (Avoid folding too vigorously as the batter will begin to deflate.)

Pour the batter into the prepared pan, spreading evenly to the edges and corners. Bake for about 9 minutes, or until the cake has risen and is light golden brown.

Meanwhile, spread a clean kitchen towel onto a flat work surface or large wire rack and dust with confectioners' sugar. When the cake is done, immediately turn it out onto the kitchen towel,

CONTINUED

peel off the parchment paper, and, using a serrated knife, trim about ⅛ to ¼ inch off of the edges. Starting at one of the short ends, roll the cake in the towel to form a cylinder and set aside to cool completely on a wire rack. (You can wrap the cake in plastic wrap at this point and set it aside at room temperature for several hours.)

Carefully unroll the cake and set it on a flat work surface. Frost the cake with chestnut buttercream, spreading it to the edges. Roll the cake once again, beginning at one of the short ends, to form a log. Set the log, seam-side down, on the work surface. Using a serrated knife and cutting on the diagonal, cut about a 3-inch piece from one of the ends. Spread some of the chocolate buttercream on top of the log (in the middle or toward one of the ends is fine) and set the cut piece on the buttercream, flat-side down. Spread the rest of the chocolate buttercream all over the log, swirling it to create a barklike effect. Set the bûche in the refrigerator to chill for at least 30 minutes. Store any leftover chocolate buttercream in an airtight container in the refrigerator for up to 3 weeks or in the freezer for up to 3 months.

Decorate the frosted bûche with meringue mushrooms, chopped pistachios, and a sprinkling of confectioners' sugar.

Using a serrated knife, cut the bûche de Noël into about ½-inch-thick slices and serve.

CHESTNUT & CHOCOLATE
Buttercreams

3½ cups (about ½ recipe) Dede's Italian Buttercream (page 135) at room temperature
¼ cup chestnut spread or sweetened chestnut purée
½ teaspoon vanilla extract
2 ounces bittersweet or semisweet chocolate, chopped

Put the buttercream in the bowl of an electric mixer fitted with the whisk attachment and whip on medium-high speed until smooth and glossy.

TO MAKE THE CHESTNUT BUTTERCREAM
Put the chestnut spread and vanilla extract in a medium bowl. Add about 1½ cups of the buttercream (reserving the remainder in the mixing bowl) and, using a wire whisk, whip until smooth.

TO MAKE THE CHOCOLATE BUTTERCREAM
Put the chocolate in a small, heatproof bowl. Set the bowl over a saucepan filled with about 1½ inches of simmering water (being sure not to let the bottom of the bowl touch the water) and stir occasionally until the chocolate is melted and smooth. Remove the bowl from the saucepan and set aside to cool to lukewarm, 7 to 10 minutes. (You can also melt the chocolate in the microwave, heating it at about 20-second intervals and stirring periodically until it is melted and smooth.)

Pour the melted chocolate into the remaining 2 cups of buttercream (reserved in the mixing bowl) and whip on medium-high speed until smooth.

Meringue Mushrooms

MAKES 1 CUP OF MERINGUE
OR 20 MUSHROOMS

2 large egg whites
½ cup confectioners' sugar

    Royal Icing (page 136) or Dede's Italian Butter
       cream (page 135) for gluing
    Natural or Dutch-process cocoa powder
       for dusting (optional)

Position a rack in the middle of the oven and preheat the oven to 200°F. Line a baking sheet with parchment paper.

Combine the egg whites and sugar in the bowl of an electric mixer fitted with the whisk attachment and whip on high speed to glossy, medium-stiff peaks. (Because this is such a small amount of meringue, you can also prepare it using a handheld mixer.)

Scrape the meringue into a piping bag fitted with a round tip (a Number 6 tip works well). Pipe the meringue into about 1-inch rounds and about 1-inch-tall cylinders directly onto the parchment paper–lined baking sheet. Bake for about 1 hour, or until the meringues are firm and still pure white.

Set the meringues on a wire rack to cool on the baking sheets.

Attach the rounds (tops) and cylinders (stems) with small dabs of royal icing and set aside to dry completely. Dust the tops with cocoa powder, if desired. Store the meringues in an airtight container for up to 2 days if using buttercream or up to 3 weeks if using royal icing. Rainy weather or a humid environment will cause them to soften quickly.

Having spent years baking gingerbread, I one day wondered, "Why confine it to the oven?" The range of gingerbread cakes and cookies is so deliciously broad that I felt sure this spicy genre could apply to an even wider range of sweets. Our fondness for gingerbread, after all, comes from more than just the moistness of a cake or the crispness of a cookie. It is the flavorful combination of such ingredients as molasses, brown sugar, honey, and spices that ultimately defines gingerbread and, what's more, connotes the comfort and warmth we associate with old-fashioned sweets.

CHAPTER FOUR: Ice Creams & Confections

The following recipes might surprise you. They don't much look like traditional gingerbread, but their spicy sweetness will remind you of it just the same. From rich ice cream and fruit-filled panforte to buttery caramels and tender toffee, the cakes and cookies we love have inspired a new category of satisfying gingerbread treats.

I must say, it is a truly wild and wonderful thing, this gingerbread ice cream. Reinterpreting a dessert we usually experience in its soft cakey or crispy form as lusciously rich, cold, and creamy is, at least for me, transformative. This ice cream turns the whole concept of gingerbread upside down, and in a deliciously comforting way. Gingerbread ice cream is not just a spiced-up version of vanilla. It derives its complexity and depth of flavor from a deliberate layering of ingredients. First, the milk and cream are infused with fresh ginger to create a fragrant, gingery base. Next, brown sugar and molasses contribute the quintessential gingerbready quality. Finally, a generous amount of spice and vanilla adds requisite warmth and perfume to the custard. This is particularly important, since we experience the gingerbread flavor less intensely once the custard freezes. Who knew you could make gingerbread without an oven?

Gingerbread Ice Cream

MAKES ABOUT 1¼ QUARTS

1½ cups heavy (whipping) cream

1½ cups whole milk

One 3- to 4-inch piece fresh ginger (about 1¼ ounces), peeled and roughly chopped

6 large egg yolks

½ cup packed light brown sugar

¼ cup molasses

2 teaspoons ground ginger

2 teaspoons ground cinnamon

½ teaspoon ground cloves

½ teaspoon freshly grated nutmeg

¼ teaspoon salt

2 teaspoons vanilla extract

Stir together the cream, milk, and fresh ginger in a medium (at least 2-quart) saucepan and bring to a boil over medium-high heat. Remove from the heat and set aside to infuse for 30 minutes to 1 hour.

Strain the cream and milk, discarding the ginger. Return the infused mixture to the saucepan and again bring to a boil over medium-high heat.

Meanwhile, whisk together the egg yolks, brown sugar, molasses, ginger, cinnamon, cloves, nutmeg, and salt in a large bowl until thick and smooth.

As soon as the cream mixture comes to a boil, gradually drizzle it into the egg yolk mixture while whisking constantly. (Adding the hot milk too quickly will cause the egg yolks to curdle.)

Pour the mixture back into the pan and cook over low heat, stirring constantly with a wooden spoon, until it thickens and coats the back of the spoon. (Watch carefully here, as it curdles very quickly after reaching the right thickness. Better to remove it from the heat too early than too late.) Strain the custard into a medium bowl and stir in the vanilla extract. Set the bowl of custard in a larger bowl of ice water and set aside to cool, stirring occasionally, for about 20 minutes. Cover the custard with plastic wrap and set in the refrigerator to chill completely, at least 4 hours or overnight.

Pour the mixture into an ice cream machine and process according to the manufacturer's directions. Spoon the ice cream into a freezer-safe, airtight container and freeze until firm, at least 1 hour.

Serve generous scoops of the ice cream in bowls or coupe dishes.

I first experienced caramel ice cream years ago while working in a French restaurant outside of Philadelphia. Preparing the custard seemed nothing less than high culinary drama, featuring burning sugar, scalding cream, and a bowl of unsuspecting egg yolks. Watching the pastry chef at the stove, minding his large beat-up pots of bubbling brew, was like witnessing a focused alchemist in his fire-lit laboratory. At just the right moment, the chef conjoined the disparate elements of cream and sugar, and his battle with the lava-like caramel ensued. The mixture spat and sputtered and threatened to rise out of the pot, but the chef soon took charge. Stealthily approaching the fiery sugar, wooden spoon in hand, he deftly stirred the caramel into submission. When the ferocious bubbling had settled, the chef whisked the still piping-hot caramel into the egg yolks and returned the tamed custard to the pot. He then traded his whisk for a gentler long, wooden spoon. Displaying an assuredness that comes only from years of coaching fickle custards that have a tendency to go lumpy into smooth successes, he began rhythmically stirring the capricious caramel mixture. Within minutes, the transformation was complete. The chef had lulled the already creamy custard into super-rich, velvety lusciousness. He set the thick, amber-colored cream in the refrigerator to chill for several hours and then delegated the final task to the kitchen's dishwasher-size ice cream machine. The last of the transmutations was complete in no time. There was only one thing left to do. The chef—part alchemist, part epicure, part ice cream superhero—presented me with a generous scoop of frozen caramel perfection. Although making caramel ice cream is certainly less intimidating to me now, it really is no less magical. I think you'll find this version quite manageable and consistently successful. Just be careful around the hot sugar and cook it in at least a 2-quart saucepan. You want to be sure that when you add the cream and it bubbles up, the caramel won't pour out all over your stove. Nothing is needed to improve this ice cream, but why not try? Spicy, chewy ginger cookies and mounds of smooth chocolate ganache mingle gorgeously with the sweet, slightly bitter flavor and velvety texture of the ice cream. Of course, if you want, leave the cookies and chocolate out entirely. Serve the ice cream as an accompaniment to warm gingerbread or simply on its own.

Caramel–Ginger Cookie–Chocolate Chunk Ice Cream

MAKES ABOUT 1½ QUARTS

2 cups heavy (whipping) cream
1 cup whole milk
1 cup sugar
¼ cup water
6 large egg yolks
¼ teaspoon salt

2 teaspoons vanilla extract
12 Logan's Favorite Soft Molasses Cookies (page 53),
    or about 6 Giant Chewy Ginger Cookies (page 52),
    or soft store-bought molasses cookies, as needed
½ cup (about ¼ recipe) Bittersweet Chocolate Ganache
    (facing page), firm but at room temperature

Stir together the cream and milk in a medium saucepan and bring to a boil over medium-high heat.

Meanwhile, stir together the sugar and water in a medium (at least 2-quart), heavy-bottomed (preferably stainless-steel) saucepan. Cook over low to medium-low heat until the caramel is dark amber in color. (Do not stir the caramel as it cooks, as this will potentially cause it to crystallize.)

Remove the caramel from the heat and carefully pour in about ¼ cup of the hot cream mixture. The caramel will bubble fiercely, so do this slowly. Gradually add the rest of the cream in about ¼-cup increments, stirring until combined. (The caramel should dissolve easily in the hot cream, but if you find that some of it hardens into small bits, stir the mixture over medium-low heat until the caramel is completely melted again.)

Whisk together the egg yolks and salt in a large bowl until smooth. Gradually drizzle the hot caramel cream into the egg yolks while whisking constantly. (Adding the hot cream too quickly will cause the egg yolks to curdle.) Pour the mixture back into the pan and cook over low heat, stirring constantly with a wooden spoon, until it thickens and coats the back of the spoon. (Watch carefully here, as it curdles very quickly after reaching the right thickness. Better to remove it from the heat too early than too late.) Strain the custard into a medium bowl and stir in the vanilla extract. Set the bowl of custard in a larger bowl of ice water and set aside to cool, stirring occasionally, for about 20 minutes. Cover the custard with plastic wrap and set in the refrigerator to chill completely, at least 4 hours or overnight.

Pour the mixture into an ice cream machine and process according to the manufacturer's directions.

Break the cookies into pieces and stir them, along with teaspoon-size mounds of ganache, into the finished ice cream while it is still soft. Spoon the ice cream into a freezer-safe, air-tight container and freeze until firm, at least 1 hour.

Serve generous scoops of the ice cream in bowls or coupe dishes.

Chocolate Ganache

MAKES ABOUT 2 CUPS

10 ounces bittersweet chocolate, finely chopped
1 cup plus 2 tablespoons heavy (whipping) cream

Put the chocolate in a large bowl. Pour the cream into a small saucepan and bring to a boil over medium-high heat. Pour the cream over the chocolate, set aside for about 1 minute until the cream softens the chocolate, then stir until smooth. If the chocolate doesn't melt completely, heat the ganache in the microwave at about 10-second intervals until completely smooth.

Use immediately as a coating or sauce, or, for truffles, chill it in the refrigerator until firm. If you are using the ganache later, pour it into an airtight container, set aside until cool, and store in the refrigerator for up to 1 month.

To melt the ganache once it becomes firm, put it in a large, heat-proof bowl. Set the bowl over a sauce-pan filled with about 1½ inches of simmering water (being sure not to let the bottom of the bowl touch the water) and stir occasionally until the ganache is melted and smooth. Remove the bowl from the saucepan and set aside to cool slightly, about 10 minutes. (You can also melt the ganache in the microwave, heating it at about 20-second intervals and stirring periodically until it is melted and smooth.)

When I was developing recipes for *pain d'épices* (French spice bread), I had an idea that this spicy, honey-sweetened bread would be wonderful in ice cream. When I learned that Anne Willan had not only already thought of this, but also included a recipe for Spice Bread Ice Cream in her book *Anne Willan: From My Château Kitchen*, I realized my culinary revelation was not quite so impressive after all. In fact, as Anne explains, Burgundian chefs have been flavoring ice cream with leftover pain d'épices crumbs for some time. Although my version of pain d'épices ice cream might not be completely unique within the genre, I still think it's pretty special. Reflecting the character of the bread itself, the custard is sweetened with honey, flavored with a typical array of Burgundian spices, and infused with orange. Then, once frozen but still soft, Grand Marnier-moistened cubes of toasted pain d'épices are folded into this vibrantly perfumed base. The result is a cold, creamy, chewy, spicy, and sweet dessert that captures the very essence of an autumnal Burgundian kitchen.

➤ Pain d'Épices Ice Cream ◄

MAKES ABOUT 1½ QUARTS

1½ cups heavy (whipping) cream

1½ cups whole milk

2 pieces fresh orange peel (approximately 3 inches long and 1 inch wide), plus 1 teaspoon grated orange zest

6 large egg yolks

½ cup honey

¼ cup sugar

½ teaspoon ground ginger

½ teaspoon ground cinnamon

¼ teaspoon ground cloves

¼ teaspoon ground aniseed

¼ teaspoon salt

1 teaspoon vanilla extract

1 loaf (½ recipe) day-old Pain d'Épices (page 115)

3 tablespoons Grand Marnier, Cointreau, or other orange-flavored liquer

Stir together the cream, milk, and orange peel in a medium saucepan and bring to a boil over medium-high heat. Remove from the heat and set aside to infuse for 30 to 40 minutes.

Strain the cream and milk, discarding the orange peel. Return the infused mixture to the saucepan and again bring to a boil over medium-high heat.

Meanwhile, whisk together the egg yolks, honey, sugar, ginger, cinnamon, cloves, aniseed, and salt in a large bowl until thick and smooth.

As soon as the cream mixture comes to a boil, gradually drizzle it into the egg yolk mixture while whisking constantly. (Adding

the hot milk too quickly will cause the egg yolks to curdle.) Pour the mixture back into the pan and cook over low heat, stirring constantly with a wooden spoon, until it thickens and coats the back of the spoon. (Watch carefully here, as it curdles very quickly after reaching the right thickness. Better to remove it from the heat too early than too late.) Strain the custard into a medium bowl and stir in the vanilla extract and orange zest. Set the bowl of custard in a larger bowl of ice water and set aside to cool, stirring occasionally, for about 20 minutes. Cover the custard with plastic wrap and set in the refrigerator to chill completely, at least 4 hours or overnight.

Position a rack in the middle of the oven and preheat the oven to 350°F. Line a baking sheet with parchment paper.

Using about one-quarter of the pain d'épices loaf, roughly cut the bread into about 1-inch cubes. (Reserve the rest of the loaf for another use.) Spread them out onto the prepared baking sheet and bake for about 10 minutes, or until the cubes are lightly toasted but still a bit soft. Set the cubes on a wire rack to cool on the baking sheet.

Pour the cooled custard into an ice cream machine and process according to the manufacturer's directions.

Put the pain d'épices cubes in a medium bowl and sprinkle with the Grand Marnier, tossing to coat. Fold the bread into the soft ice cream and spoon into a freezer-safe, airtight container. Freeze until firm, at least 1 hour.

Serve generous scoops of the ice cream in bowls or coupe dishes.

If you like pumpkin pie, you will love this ice cream. Smooth, rich, and creamy, it has a sweet squashy goodness that pairs perfectly with the crunchy, spicy shards of gingersnaps that permeate it. This ice cream is so comforting and flavorful, you will find yourself heading toward the freezer door even on a chilly fall afternoon. It is delicious on its own, but you can also vary the recipe slightly to suit other uses. Omit the gingersnap pieces and press spoonfuls of it between two Giant Chewy Ginger Cookies to make Gingerbread-Pumpkin Ice Cream Sandwiches (page 77). In this pure form, it is a cool and creamy accompaniment to a slice of warm gingerbread, as well.

→ Pumpkin-Gingersnap Ice Cream ←

MAKES ABOUT 1½ QUARTS

 1 cup heavy (whipping) cream
 1 cup whole milk
 ½ cup granulated sugar
 ¼ cup packed light brown sugar
 6 large egg yolks
 ½ teaspoon ground cinnamon
 ½ teaspoon ground ginger
 ¼ teaspoon freshly grated nutmeg

 ¼ teaspoon ground allspice
 ⅛ teaspoon ground cloves
 ¼ teaspoon salt
1½ teaspoons vanilla extract
 1 cup pumpkin purée
12 Old-Time Gingersnaps (page 39) or
    store-bought gingersnaps

*

Stir together the cream and milk in a medium (at least 2-quart) saucepan and bring to a boil over medium-high heat.

Meanwhile, whisk together the granulated and brown sugars, egg yolks, cinnamon, ginger, nutmeg, allspice, cloves, and salt in a large bowl until thick and smooth.

As soon as the cream mixture comes to a boil, gradually drizzle it into the egg yolk mixture while whisking constantly. (Adding the hot cream too quickly will cause the egg yolks to curdle.) Pour the mixture back into the pan and cook over low heat, stirring constantly with a wooden spoon, until it thickens and coats the back of the spoon. (Watch carefully here, as it curdles very quickly after reaching the right thickness. Better to remove it from the heat too early than too late.) Strain the custard into a medium bowl and stir in the vanilla extract. Set the bowl of custard in a larger bowl of ice water and set aside to cool, stirring occasionally, for about 20 minutes. Cover the custard with plastic wrap and set in the refrigerator to chill completely, at least 4 hours or overnight.

Whisk the pumpkin purée into the chilled custard. Pour the mixture into an ice cream machine and process according to the manufacturer's directions.

Break the gingersnaps into pieces and stir them into the finished ice cream while it is still soft. Spoon the ice cream into a freezer-safe, airtight container and freeze until firm, at least 1 hour.

Serve generous scoops of the ice cream in bowls or coupe dishes.

Years ago I gave a series of baking demonstrations to a group of elderly ladies at an assisted-living facility. On the day of my first class, I arrived early to find one of the women already in the activities room waiting for me. She smiled and greeted me in a friendly voice as though she knew me. It turns out she did. Mrs. Sarah Adamson had been my fourth-grade teacher. Once tall and statuesque with her waist-long blonde hair piled elegantly into a large bun, she seemed to me now like a delicate and fragile flower. She was confined to a wheelchair and wore her bobbed hair tucked neatly under a headband. During her last year in the home, Mrs. Adamson shared her notebooks of handwritten recipes with me, one of which was for bourbon balls. Like many versions of this confection, Mrs. Adamson's recipe for these nutty little gems calls for crushed vanilla wafers, confectioners' sugar, corn syrup, cocoa powder, walnuts, and a douse of strong whiskey. In memory of my dear teacher, I have developed a gingerbread variation that makes use of leftover ginger cookies. Hazelnuts contribute texture, while honey adds a pleasant floral sweetness. I have also replaced the whiskey with rum, just because I like it, but you can use whiskey if you prefer. These powdery little treats make great gifts (for grown-up friends, especially, given the rum "punch"). They are quite pretty and store well, too, the flavors marrying and mellowing over time. I think Mrs. Adamson would be pleased with my take on an old favorite.

Gingerbread-Hazelnut Rum Balls

MAKES ABOUT 35 BALLS

2½ cups (about 30 whole) ground Old-Time Gingersnaps (page 39) or store-bought gingersnaps

2 tablespoons natural cocoa powder

1 cup confectioners' sugar, plus more for rolling

1 cup hazelnuts, toasted, skinned, and finely chopped

4 to 6 tablespoons honey

4 to 6 tablespoons rum or whiskey

Stir together the ground gingersnaps, cocoa powder, 1 cup confectioners' sugar, and nuts in a large bowl. Pour in the honey and rum, stirring until the mixture is evenly moistened, slightly sticky, and holds together when you squeeze a bit in your hand. (If the mixture seems too dry, add a bit more honey and/or rum.)

With slightly damp hands, shape the mixture into walnut-size balls and roll in confectioners' sugar.

Serve the rum balls immediately, or store them for at least several days, as they improve with age. Store the rum balls, with or without the sugar coating, in an airtight container, layered between sheets of parchment or waxed paper, in a cool area for up to 3 weeks.

I have eighteenth-century cookery book author Amelia Simmons to thank for inspiring this confection. In her 1796 cookbook, *American Cookery*—the first cookbook authored by an American—she included two spiced Butter Drop cakes (cookies, really) among her no less than five gingerbread recipes. My version of these buttery morsels indeed puts me in mind of the small spice cakes and sugary confections that adorned dessert tables in Europe and America centuries ago. Usually arranged on silver or glass *épergnes* or *surtouts de tables* (ornamented center dishes), sweetmeats of this kind were as visually dazzling as they were celebrations of the confectioner's skill. Cloaked elegantly in sheer white glaze, these petite treats would have been well suited to a gleaming eighteenth-century silver dish or glistening cut-glass tray. Fortunately, these ten-der little rounds, flavored delicately with lemon and spice, are easier to prepare today than they might have been centuries ago. The dough comes together quickly and requires no chilling before shaping and baking. The glaze (which often seems daunting but really isn't) is also a snap and only requires whisking together a handful of ingredients. Served for dessert, as part of a petit four tray, or packaged as gifts, these butter drops offer a unique and elegant twist on traditional dark gingerbread.

Gingerbread Butter Drops WITH LEMON GLAZE

MAKES 32 BUTTER DROPS

1³/₄ cups all-purpose flour

¹/₄ teaspoon salt

1 teaspoon ground ginger

¹/₂ teaspoon ground cinnamon

¹/₄ teaspoon freshly grated nutmeg

³/₄ cup (1¹/₂ sticks) unsalted butter at room temperature

¹/₂ cup confectioners' sugar

1 tablespoon heavy (whipping) cream, plus more as needed

¹/₂ teaspoon lemon extract or oil

LEMON GLAZE

4¹/₂ cups confectioners' sugar

6 tablespoons light corn syrup

¹/₄ cup hot water

5 tablespoons freshly squeezed lemon juice

¹/₄ teaspoon lemon extract or lemon oil (optional)

Royal Icing (page 136) for decorating (optional)

Position a rack in the middle of the oven and preheat the oven to 325°F. Line a large baking sheet with parchment paper.

Whisk together the flour, salt, ginger, cinnamon, and nutmeg in a medium bowl.

Put the butter in the bowl of an electric mixer fitted with the paddle attachment and beat on medium-high speed until smooth. Gradually add the confectioners' sugar and continue beating until light and fluffy. Incorporate the cream and lemon extract, mixing until smooth. Reduce the mixing speed to low and gradually add the flour mixture, mixing just until the dough comes together. (The dough should form a fairly moist clump when you squeeze a bit in your hand. If it seems too crumbly, mix in additional cream, about 1 teaspoon at a time, until you're satisfied.)

Turn the dough out onto a flat work surface and shape into a cylinder about 3 inches in diameter. Divide the dough into quarters. Divide each piece into quarters again, and then cut each of those pieces in half, creating 32 pieces. Roll the pieces into balls and arrange them on the prepared baking sheet

CONTINUED

about 1½ inches apart. (The butter drops expand slightly during baking.) Press the balls lightly so they stay put and don't roll around on the sheet.

Bake the butter drops for about 20 minutes, or until they are very light golden brown. Cool the butter drops on the baking sheets set on wire racks for about 2 minutes before removing them to the racks to cool completely. (You can store the butter drops at this point in airtight containers for up to 5 days, or proceed to coat them with glaze.)

TO MAKE THE GLAZE

Whisk together the confectioners' sugar, corn syrup, hot water, lemon juice, and lemon extract (if desired) in a large bowl until smooth. Warm the glaze in the microwave at about 10-second intervals until it is just barely warm to the touch. (Warming the glaze will loosen it a bit and make it easier to coat the butter drops).

Arrange the cooled butter drops on a large wire rack set over a large baking sheet or sheet of aluminum foil. Drop the butter drops, one at a time, into the glaze, turning them with a fork to coat them completely. Using the fork, lift the butter drops out of the glaze, tap gently on the edge of the bowl to remove any excess glaze, and return them to the wire rack. Warm the glaze again in the microwave, if necessary, about halfway through the batch. After the butter drops have dried for about 5 minutes, gently reposition them on the rack, using a clean fork or paring knife, to prevent the glaze from clumping at the bases. Set the coated butter drops aside in a dry, cool area until the glaze is firm, about 45 minutes. Coat the butter drops a second time in the same manner, warming the glaze again to loosen it. (Store any leftover glaze in an airtight container in the refrigerator for up to 3 days.)

To decorate the butter drops, pipe dots or swirls of royal icing on top of the butter drops, if desired. Set aside to dry completely, about 1 hour. (Store the butter drops in an airtight container, layered between sheets of parchment or waxed paper, for up to 1 week.)

My love for gingerbread has taken me on many culinary journeys. Most recently, it has led me to this celebrated confection from Siena, Italy. *Panforte* (literally "strong bread"), like its close relation *pan pepato* (literally "peppered/spiced bread"), is quite different from American molasses-based gingerbread cake. It is actually more akin to a dense fruitcake, flavored as it is with nuts, dried fruit, honey, caramelized sugar, and spices. Panforte is most often baked in large rounds, varying from ½ inch to about 1½ inches thick, and then cut into thin wedges. In Siena, it is served (especially at Christmas) as a snack or dessert with a sweet wine, such as *vin santo*. My version includes ingredients commonly found in *panforte Margherita*, such as honey, orange zest, and almonds, but I have also added some of my own favorites: hazelnuts, walnuts, dried cranberries, and dried apricots. Enjoy slices of this colorful, chewy confection alone or with a cheese course. To make your Sienese experience complete, pair the panforte with a glass of vin santo or other luscious dessert wine.

→ Panforte Margherita ←

MAKES ONE 8-INCH PANFORTE

³/₄ cup all-purpose flour

¼ teaspoon salt

1 teaspoon ground cinnamon

½ teaspoon ground ginger

½ teaspoon ground coriander

¼ teaspoon ground allspice

⅛ teaspoon ground cloves

1 cup almonds, toasted and coarsely chopped

½ cup hazelnuts, toasted, skinned, and coarsely chopped

½ cup walnuts, toasted and coarsely chopped

1 cup lightly packed dried pitted apricots, coarsely chopped

1 cup dark raisins

³/₄ cup dried cranberries

¼ cup chopped Candied Orange Peel (page 138) or store-bought candied orange peel

2 tablespoons chopped candied citron

³/₄ cup sugar

³/₄ cup honey

¼ cup water

Confectioners' sugar for dusting

Position a rack in the middle of the oven and preheat the oven to 300ºF. Butter an 8-by-2-inch nonstick springform pan and line the bottom with parchment paper. (A nonstick pan is important here.)

Whisk together the flour, salt, cinnamon, ginger, coriander, allspice, and cloves in a large bowl. Add the almonds, hazelnuts, walnuts, dried apricots, raisins, dried cranberries, and the candied orange peel and citron, stirring to coat them evenly with the dry ingredients.

Combine the sugar, honey, and water in a small saucepan and cook over medium heat, stirring occasionally, until the sugar and honey have dissolved. Bring to a boil, place a candy thermometer in the mixture, and continue to cook, without stirring, to 238ºF (soft-ball stage), 10 to 15 minutes.

Remove the cooked sugar from the heat, immediately pour it over the nut and fruit mixture, and stir until the ingredients are well combined. The batter will be very sticky and thick.

Scrape the batter into the prepared pan and, using a heatproof spatula or your fingers, spread it evenly in the pan, pressing firmly.

CONTINUED

(If you use your fingers, you might want to wet them with cold water before you start spreading the dough to prevent them from sticking.) Wrap the pan with a parchment collar that rises about 3 inches above the pan and secure with kitchen twine.

Set the filled pan on a baking sheet and bake the panforte for 1 hour to 1 hour and 10 minutes, or until it is puffed and dark golden brown. Set the panforte on a wire rack to cool completely in the pan. When it has cooled, carefully remove the sides of the springform pan and slide the panforte off of the bottom of the pan.

Dust the panforte with confectioners' sugar and cut it into thin wedges, if serving immediately. Alternatively, omit the dusting of sugar, keep the panforte whole, and store it for at least several days, as it improves with age. To store the panforte for more than a few days, wrap it in plastic wrap and set in a cool area or in the refrigerator for at least 3 days and up to 1 month. Dust with confectioners' sugar before serving.

These days, pastry shops throughout Siena and Tuscany prepare many varieties of panforte. Panforte Margherita, however, remains one of the most traditional versions. Allegedly named for Queen Margherita (yes, same as the pizza) in the late nineteenth century, this confection calls for a flavorful combination of almonds, candied citrus, candied citron, honey, and a variety of spices, including cinnamon, allspice, ginger, and coriander. A generous dusting of confectioners' sugar adds an elegant final flourish.

It might seem rather a stretch, including caramels in a book about gingerbread. The fact of the matter is, though, that in France (and in Burgundy, in particular) the use of spices is so ubiquitous that they make their way into everything from breads and cakes to preserves and confections. This recipe is based on caramels I first experienced in the Burgundian hill town of Vézelay. The shops there were filled with tempting local specialties. Among the shelves of wine, honey, mustard, and preserves, I almost always found pretty little sacks of *caramels d'épices*. These delicious, dark amber–colored gems, wrapped beautifully in gold and purple foil, were a revelation. Spicy, sweet, and creamy, *caramels d'épices* were candy bliss. As soon as I returned home, I began developing my own recipe for these caramels, which I now present to you. I realize that making candy can be quite intimidating and admit that it is often a tricky business. These caramels, though, are truly as consistently easy to prepare as they are delicious. Encase them individually in foil or waxed paper, or wrap the entire sheet in plastic wrap, store it in a cool and dry area, and cut the caramel into pieces as you need them.

Burgundian Spiced Caramels

MAKES ONE 9-BY-5-BY-3-INCH PAN OF CARAMEL OR ABOUT FORTY-FIVE 1-INCH PIECES

1¼ cups heavy (whipping) cream
¼ cup (½ stick) unsalted butter, cut into pieces
1½ cups packed light brown sugar
¼ cup light corn syrup
¾ teaspoon ground ginger

½ teaspoon ground cinnamon
⅛ teaspoon ground allspice
⅛ teaspoon salt
1 teaspoon vanilla extract

Lightly butter a 9-by-5-by-3-inch loaf pan. Cut 2 strips of parchment paper to line the bottom and sides of the pan, allowing at least 1 inch to hang over the edges. Fit the strips into the pan, and then butter the parchment paper.

Combine the cream, butter, brown sugar, and corn syrup in a medium saucepan and cook, stirring occasionally, over medium heat until the butter is melted. Bring to a boil, place a candy thermometer in the mixture, and continue to cook the caramel, without stirring, to 248ºF (firm-ball stage), about 20 minutes. The caramel will appear foamy and dark amber in color when it is ready.

Remove the caramel from the heat and carefully stir in the ginger, cinnamon, allspice, salt, and vanilla extract. Pour the caramel evenly into the prepared pan and set aside on a wire rack to cool completely, at least 2 hours.

Lift the sheet of caramel out of the pan, using the edges of parchment, if necessary. Cut the caramel into squares or rectangles and wrap in waxed paper or candy foil. Store the caramels in an airtight container in a cool area for up to 1 month. Alternatively, wrap the whole sheet of caramel in plastic wrap and store in the refrigerator for up to 6 weeks, cutting pieces as needed.

I never had success making toffee until my husband's friend Alison (quite a skilled toffee maker) shared her recipe with me. It's not a difficult process, but I somehow managed to throw enough overcooked, greasy, or rock-hard toffee in the trash over the years that I thought maybe I was missing the toffee-making gene. Needless to say, I was thrilled when Alison's recipe worked perfectly the first time without a fuss. I have altered it a bit, adding brown sugar, spices, and vanilla to create a gingerbread version, but I owe the success of the basic recipe to Alison. This toffee is firm, but also luxuriously tender enough to melt in your mouth. The key is to watch the sugar mixture carefully as it cooks. Once you place the candy thermometer in the pan, stand at or near the stove as the toffee bubbles and thickens. This is not the time to start doing dishes or answer the phone, as the mercury zooms to the final temperature during the last few minutes of cooking. This toffee is pretty enough to serve at Christmas, but, really, it is so delicious that I make it year-round. The chocolate coating and sprinkling of green pistachios and red dried cherries add complexity of flavor and texture, as well as celebratory panache. Serve the shardlike pieces in an attractive dish, or place them in cellophane bags tied with ribbon for tasty gifts.

Spiced Christmas Toffee

MAKES 1½ POUNDS

1 cup (2 sticks) unsalted butter
3/4 cup granulated sugar
1/4 cup packed light brown sugar
1 tablespoon light corn syrup
3 tablespoons water
1½ teaspoons ground ginger

1/2 teaspoon ground cinnamon
1/4 teaspoon ground cloves
1 teaspoon vanilla extract
6 ounces bittersweet chocolate, chopped
1/2 cup shelled toasted pistachios, roughly chopped
1/2 cup dried cherries, roughly chopped

Line a 13-by-9-by-2-inch baking dish or pan with aluminum foil, allowing the foil to extend about 1 inch over the sides.

Butter the sides of a heavy-bottomed, 2-quart saucepan. Put the butter in the pan and heat over medium heat until melted. Stir in the granulated and brown sugars, corn syrup, and water and bring to a boil. Place a candy thermometer in the mixture and cook the toffee, without stirring, to 290ºF (soft-crack stage), about 10 minutes. (Watch carefully as it approaches the final temperature.)

Remove the toffee from the heat and quickly, but carefully, stir in the ginger, cinnamon, cloves, and vanilla extract. (Be careful, as the toffee might spit a bit when the cool extract hits the hot mixture.) Pour the toffee evenly into the prepared baking dish and set aside for about 5 minutes, or until it begins to harden.

Sprinkle the chopped chocolate evenly over the hot toffee and let it sit for about 30 seconds, or until the chocolate begins to melt. Using a spoon or spatula, carefully spread the melting chocolate over the toffee. (All of the chocolate should be melted within a couple of minutes.) Sprinkle the pistachios and cherries over the top and set aside on a wire rack in a cool area or in the refrigerator until the toffee is firm, about 1 hour.

Lift the firm toffee out of the baking dish, using the edges of the foil, if necessary. Carefully peel away the foil and break the toffee into shardlike pieces. Store the toffee in an airtight container, layered between sheets of parchment or waxed paper, in a cool area or in the refrigerator for up to 3 weeks.

Why wait for dessert to eat gingerbread? There are plenty of hours in the day, so why not start at breakfast? Truth be told, these recipes do not call for cutting rich cakes or crumbling cookies into cereal bowls first thing in the morning. I must admit, however, that I happily advocate serving dishes of toasted day-old gingerbread, sweetened with a sprinkling of turbinado sugar, and moistened with a healthy drizzle of milk or cream. This improvisational recipe reminds me of a fox-fur hat I own—fluffy and soft, but I don't wear it often. When I do, it makes me feel chic and slightly decadent in a charmingly old-fashioned sort of way. Why can't a bit of leftover cake have the same effect?

CHAPTER FIVE: Gingerbread for Breakfast

It is no wonder that gingerbread translates beautifully into all sorts of breakfast items. Vibrant, sweet, and often served warm, these early-morning gingerbreads will entice even the most bleary-eyed diner. The following pancakes, waffles, doughnuts, and scones will certainly be familiar to you, but they become even more satisfying with warm infusions of spices, brown sugar, and molasses. The recipes for pain d'épices and pain d'épices French toast might be less recognizable as gingerbread goes, but I suspect you will soon find them enticing additions to your breakfast repertoire. Flavored with citrus, honey, and spices, including the licorice-perfumed aniseed, this Burgundian spice bread is quite different from American gingerbread. It is bound, however, to become a welcome addition to your breakfast table just the same. I hope serving gingerbread for breakfast will inspire your culinary routine. Who knows? You just might want to prepare these recipes at other times of the day, too.

If you like pancakes (and, heck, who doesn't?), I suspect you will very much enjoy these gingerbread darlings. The addition of whole-wheat flour lends a complexity and nuttiness to the pancakes without making them dense and heavy. The warm wheatiness buoys the molasses quality of the brown sugar and the intensity of the spices, enhancing the overall gingerbread quality. These mahogany beauties are only mildly sweet and pleasantly bright with a bit of orange zest. This batter comes together quickly, although be sure to plan ahead, as it needs to rest in the refrigerator for 3 to 6 hours.

Gingerbread Pancakes

MAKES 3½ CUPS BATTER, OR FOURTEEN 4-INCH PANCAKES

1¼ cups whole-wheat flour
⅓ cup all-purpose flour
¼ cup packed dark brown sugar
1½ teaspoons baking powder
¾ teaspoon salt
1 teaspoon ground cinnamon
¾ teaspoon ground ginger
½ teaspoon ground cloves
¼ teaspoon freshly grated nutmeg

1 teaspoon grated orange zest
1 large egg
2 cups whole milk
2 teaspoons vanilla extract
5½ tablespoons unsalted butter, 3 tablespoons melted

Apple Butter (page 17) for serving (optional)
Maple syrup for serving (optional)

Whisk together the whole-wheat flour, all-purpose flour, brown sugar, baking powder, salt, cinnamon, ginger, cloves, nutmeg, and orange zest in a large bowl.

Whisk together the egg, milk, vanilla extract, and melted butter in a medium bowl until combined. Pour the egg mixture into the flour mixture and whisk just until combined. (Avoid mixing the batter too thoroughly; some lumps are okay.) Cover the bowl with plastic wrap and set in the refrigerator to chill and rest for at least 3 hours or overnight.

Using the remaining 2½ tablespoons of butter, heat about 1 teaspoon in a large sauté pan or skillet over medium heat. (A nonstick pan is helpful here.) Pour ¼ cup of batter into the pan for each pancake. (Depending on the size of the pan, you will want to make about two at a time.) Cook for about 2 minutes, or until bubbles appear on the surface of the cakes and they begin to brown ever so slightly around the edges. Flip the cakes and cook on the other sides for about 2 minutes more.

Remove the pancakes immediately to a serving plate, or set them on a baking sheet to keep warm in the oven (see Note). Carefully wipe the pan with a paper towel, melt another teaspoon of butter, and continue the process with the rest of the batter.

To serve, spread the warm pancakes with a layer of Apple Butter and/or drizzle with maple syrup, if desired.

NOTE
If you want to prepare all of the pancakes before serving, position a rack in the middle of the oven and preheat the oven to 200°F. Line a baking sheet with aluminum foil. Place the just-cooked pancakes on the baking sheet, layering them between sheets of parchment paper, and set them in the oven to keep warm.

These gingerbread waffles are as flavorful and comforting as they are easy to prepare. Tender and moist, they are a far cry from the crisp, airy waffles that often fail to satisfy. Pumpkin and gingerbread are deliciously symbiotic. Here, the pumpkin adds a warm, sweet undertone to the spicy, intense molasses flavor of these dark chestnut-colored treats. The addition of vanilla sugar only improves the eating experience, as the sandy, crunchy sugar complements the soft, supple waffles. You might want to alter the cooking method, depending on the size of your waffle iron. My 7-inch round iron holds between ³/₄ cup and 1 cup of batter. The latter amount results in a high, thick waffle, but it does have a tendency to escape out of the sides of the iron. Use your own discretion in these waffle-making matters and cook the amount that is best suited to your iron and clean-up routine.

→ Gingerbread-Pumpkin Waffles WITH VANILLA SUGAR ←

MAKES 3 CUPS BATTER, OR THREE TO FOUR 7-INCH ROUND WAFFLES

³/₄ cup all-purpose flour
3 tablespoons granulated sugar
2 teaspoons baking powder
¹/₂ teaspoon salt
1¹/₂ teaspoons ground ginger
1 teaspoon ground cinnamon
³/₄ teaspoon ground cloves
¹/₂ teaspoon freshly ground nutmeg

¹/₄ cup pumpkin purée
3 large eggs
1¹/₄ cups whole milk
3 tablespoons unsalted butter, melted and cooled
2 tablespoons dark molasses
2 teaspoons vanilla extract

Vanilla Sugar (recipe follows) for coating

Preheat a waffle iron on the highest setting.

Whisk together the flour, sugar, baking powder, salt, ginger, cinnamon, cloves, and nutmeg in a large bowl.

Whisk together the pumpkin purée, eggs, milk, butter, molasses, and vanilla extract in a medium bowl until combined. Pour the egg mixture into the flour mixture and whisk until just combined. (Avoid mixing the batter too thoroughly; some lumps are okay.)

Pour the Vanilla Sugar into a shallow dish or pan that is big enough to accommodate the size waffles you are making. Shake the dish to spread the sugar evenly on the bottom.

Pour 3/4 to 1 cup of the batter onto the hot waffle iron (the amount will depend on the size of your iron) and cook for about

4 minutes, or until the iron ceases to steam. Carefully lift the waffle out of the iron (it will be quite tender and could break apart) and set immediately in the dish of vanilla sugar, lightly pressing the sugar into it and turning to coat. Remove the waffle immediately to a serving plate, or set it on a baking sheet to keep warm in the oven (see Note). Repeat using the rest of the batter.

Serve the waffles warm.

NOTE

If you want to prepare all of the waffles before serving, position a rack in the middle of the oven and preheat the oven to 200°F. Line a baking sheet with aluminum foil. Place the just-cooked waffles on the baking sheet, layering them between sheets of parchment paper, and set them in the oven to keep warm.

Vanilla Sugar

MAKES 1$\frac{1}{2}$ CUPS

$\frac{3}{4}$ cup granulated sugar
$\frac{1}{2}$ cup confectioners' sugar
2 teaspoons vanilla extract

Whisk together all of the ingredients in a small bowl or dish until the vanilla is evenly distributed and the mixture has a sandy consistency. Store in a sealed jar or airtight container indefinitely.

Just when you thought gingerbread couldn't get any better, here come gingerbread doughnuts. These luscious honeys are based on old-fashioned fried cake doughnuts. Can you think of a better way to treat tender rounds of cake than to bathe them in a pan of hot oil? After energetically puffing and browning in the pan, these chestnut-colored gems—moist on the inside and crisp on the outside—receive a healthy toss in cinnamon sugar to complete the treatment. Doughnuts might seem like a lot of work, but this recipe is really very simple. There are just a few things to consider before starting out. First, be sure to plan ahead and allow the sticky dough time to chill and rest before cutting it into doughnuts and doughnut holes. Because this dough is quite soft, you might even want to keep the uncooked doughnuts in the refrigerator for a bit before frying them. If they are too slack and soft, they will not fry properly. Second, maintaining the appropriate oil temperature is vital to the success of your doughnut endeavor, as it is to all frying activities. If the oil is too hot, the doughnuts will burn before the interiors are fully cooked. Oil that is too cool will result in, well, oil-laden gingerbread rocks. Use a candy thermometer to keep track of the temperature and maintain it between 360° and 375°F. Know, too, that as soon as you introduce the doughnuts into the oil, the temperature will drop. In addition, the more you fry at once, the longer it will take for the temperature to recover. Just continue fiddling with the flame and keep an avid watch. Finally, once you begin frying, let the phone ring and the e-mails gather. There will be plenty of time to attend to those things once you have a warm, sugarcoated, gingerbread doughnut in hand.

Gingerbread Doughnuts WITH CINNAMON SUGAR

MAKES ABOUT 20 DOUGHNUTS AND 20 DOUGHNUT HOLES

3³/₄ cups all-purpose flour
1 tablespoon baking powder
1¹/₄ teaspoons baking soda
1 teaspoon salt
1 teaspoon ground cinnamon
1 teaspoon ground ginger
¹/₄ teaspoon freshly grated nutmeg
¹/₄ teaspoon ground allspice
¹/₈ teaspoon ground cloves

¹/₂ cup packed light brown sugar
¹/₂ cup molasses
2 large eggs
1 teaspoon vanilla extract
6 tablespoons unsalted butter, melted and cooled
1 cup sour cream

Vegetable oil for frying
Cinnamon Sugar (recipe follows) for coating

Whisk together the flour, baking powder, baking soda, salt, cinnamon, ginger, nutmeg, allspice, and cloves in a large bowl.

Combine the brown sugar, molasses, eggs, and vanilla extract in the bowl of an electric mixer fitted with the whisk attachment and whip on medium speed until smooth. Drizzle in the butter, continuing to mix until the mixture is smooth. Incorporate the sour cream, about ¹/₂ cup at a time, stopping once or twice to scrape the sides of the bowl. Reduce the mixing speed to medium-low and gradually incorporate the flour mixture, beating until just combined. (The dough will be smooth and sticky.) Scrape the dough into a large bowl, cover with plastic wrap, and set in the refrigerator to chill and rest for at least 45 minutes or overnight.

Heat about 1½ inches of vegetable oil to 375ºF in a large, straight-sided sauté pan.

Pour the Cinnamon Sugar into a shallow dish or pan that is big enough to accommodate several doughnuts at once.

Roll the chilled dough to about ½ inch thick on a lightly floured work surface. Cut into 2½-inch rounds, and then cut out the centers, using a ⅞- or 1-inch-diameter cutter. Arrange the doughnuts on a parchment-lined baking sheet. The dough will become soft quite quickly, so, as you work, set them aside in the refrigerator to remain firm, if necessary. Roll the doughnut holes into balls and set them on a parchment-lined baking sheet, as well.

Carefully slip about 4 or 5 doughnuts at a time into the hot oil, adjusting the heat, as necessary, to maintain a frying temperature between 360º and 375ºF. Fry for about 2 minutes on each side, or until the doughnuts are well browned and puffed. Remove the doughnuts to a paper towel–lined baking sheet to drain for several minutes.

While they are still warm, drop the doughnuts in the Cinnamon Sugar, coating them liberally, and set them on a wire rack. Continue the frying process, adding more oil to the pan as necessary. Fry the doughnut holes in the same manner, for about 1½ to 2 minutes, watching them carefully as they brown more quickly than the doughnuts. Toss while still warm in the cinnamon sugar and set on a wire rack.

Serve the doughnuts and doughnut holes immediately or at room temperature. Store the cooled doughnuts in an airtight container or in a zip-top bag for up to 4 days.

Cinnamon Sugar

1½ cups granulated sugar
1½ tablespoons ground cinnamon

Stir together the sugar and cinnamon in a small bowl. Store in a jar or airtight container indefinitely.

I first tasted *pain d'épices* during a trip to France. I was traveling with a group of fellow food writers, and we had the good fortune to stay in Burgundy at Château du Feÿ—former home to cooking great Anne Willan and her cookery school, La Varenne. Pain d'épices appeared in virtually every little food shop and market we visited. We were all so intrigued with this favorite local bread that inevitably one of us would purchase a loaf for the next morning's breakfast. I still have such fond memories of sitting in Anne's seventeenth-century breakfast room with the group, drinking espresso, eating slices of warm pain d'épices spread with butter and honey, and planning the day's events. As Anne explained, pain d'épices has been a Burgundian specialty for more than six centuries. It is traditionally a yeast bread prepared with rye flour, a generous quantity of honey, and a slew of pungent spices. The large amount of sugar in the dough makes successful leavening a tricky business, though. It has a nasty propensity for killing off the yeast and thus any hopes of proper leavening. To remedy this problem, contemporary bakers are replacing rye flour with white flour and using chemical leaveners, such as baking soda and baking powder, rendering yeast obsolete. Although the methods for making pain d'épices have changed throughout the centuries, its flavors seem to have remained very much the same. If American molasses-sweetened gingerbread is warm and comforting, pain d'épices is serious and assertive. There seem to be as many varieties of this bread as there are bakers who prepare it. Some loaves are dark chestnut in color and intensely spiced, while others are light golden and mildly perfumed. All, however, are flavored with the traditional ingredients of honey, orange, and anise. Anne Willan's recipe, published in her book *From My Château Kitchen*, inspired me to create my own. Baking into moist, deep amber-colored loaves, this bread obtains a gentle sweetness from brown sugar and honey and is elegantly and warmly perfumed with orange, anise, ginger, cinnamon, and cloves. If you can refrain from slicing into these fragrant loaves right away, try to do so. Anne suggests allowing the bread to rest for a couple of days so the flavors can meld and mellow. Enjoy generous slices at room temperature or toasted, plain or spread with butter and jam. I promise, even if you've never been to Burgundy, you'll feel as though you're there.

Pain d'Épices

MAKES TWO 8½-BY-4¼-BY-3-INCH LOAVES

*

1 cup whole milk
½ cup freshly squeezed orange juice
¾ cup packed dark brown sugar
1¾ cups honey
4 cups all-purpose flour
¾ teaspoon salt
1 teaspoon ground aniseed
1 teaspoon ground ginger
¾ teaspoon ground cinnamon
¾ teaspoon ground cloves

Grated zest of 1 orange
2 tablespoons finely chopped crystallized ginger
2 large egg yolks
2 teaspoons baking soda
1 tablespoon Grand Marnier, Cointreau, or other
    orange-flavored liqueur

Unsalted butter for serving (optional)
Jam or honey for serving (optional)

CONTINUED

Begin preparing the bread at least 8 hours before baking.

Stir together the milk, orange juice, brown sugar, and honey in a small saucepan. Cook over medium-low heat, stirring occasionally, until the sugar has melted and the mixture is smooth. Remove from the heat and cool to room temperature.

Meanwhile, combine the flour, salt, aniseed, ginger, cinnamon, cloves, orange zest, and crystallized ginger in the bowl of an electric mixer fitted with the paddle attachment. Mix on low speed until the ingredients are evenly distributed. Increase the mixing speed to medium-low. Pour the cooled sugar mixture in a slow, steady stream into the flour mixture, beating to form a smooth batter, about 1 minute. Cover the bowl with plastic wrap and set aside to rest in a cool area or in the refrigerator for at least 8 hours or overnight.

Position a rack in the middle of the oven and preheat the oven to 250°F. Butter two 8½-by-4¼-by-3-inch loaf pans.

Lightly whisk together the egg yolks, baking soda, and Grand Marnier in a small bowl. Return the bowl of rested batter to the mixer fitted, again, with the paddle attachment. Begin beating the batter on medium speed and add the egg mixture, beating until smooth and stopping at least once to scrape the sides and bottom of the bowl. The batter will be quite thick and sticky.

Divide the batter between the prepared pans. Cover loosely with buttered aluminum foil or parchment paper and bake for 30 minutes. Remove the foil and continue baking for about 1½ hours, or until the loaves are deep golden brown and a skewer inserted in the centers comes out clean (a few sticky crumbs are okay, too). Set the breads on a wire rack to cool completely in the pans.

To serve, cut the bread into slices, using a serrated knife, and spread with butter and/or jam or honey, if desired. Store the loaves wrapped in plastic wrap for up to 4 days at room temperature, in the refrigerator for up to 2 weeks, or in the freezer for up to 3 months.

Here is yet another yummy use for my beloved French spice bread. I actually came up with the recipe one Sunday morning when I needed to make a hot breakfast in a hurry. The *pain d'épices* is so flavorful that only a handful of other ingredients are necessary here. Not too sweet, fragrant with orange, and pleasantly crunchy from a sprinkling of turbinado sugar, this French toast requires little else than a fork. If, however, you have the time for a bit of embellishment, a drizzle of honey or the addition of a glistening preserved apricot on the plate would make for a delicious adornment.

→ Pain d'Épices French Toast ←

MAKES 8 SLICES

2 large eggs
³/₄ cup heavy (whipping) cream
2 tablespoons granulated sugar or honey
1 teaspoon grated orange zest
Eight ¹/₄- to ¹/₂-inch-thick slices Pain d'Épices
(page 115; about one-third of a loaf)

2 tablespoons unsalted butter
¹/₂ cup turbinado sugar or other raw or coarse-textured sugar

Preserved Apricots (page 118) for serving (optional)
Honey for drizzling (optional)

Whisk together the eggs, cream, sugar, and orange zest in a medium dish or shallow pan that is big enough to accommodate several slices of bread at a time. Put 4 slices of the bread in the egg mixture, turning to coat, and set aside to soak for about 1 minute. (You only want the bread to sit briefly in the mixture, as it will become quite soggy and soft if it soaks too long.)

Put 1 tablespoon of the butter in a large sauté pan or skillet and melt over medium-high heat. (A griddle would work well, too.) Carefully lift the bread slices out of the egg mixture and put them in the pan. Cook the bread slices on each side for 1 to 2 minutes, or until golden brown. About 30 seconds before removing the toast, sprinkle each piece with turbinado sugar. Transfer the French toast to serving plates and set aside to keep warm. Repeat the process with the remaining bread slices and tablespoon of butter. (If your pan allows you to cook only 2 slices of bread at a time, just adjust the amount of butter accordingly. Also, you might want to discard any butter left in the pan between batches, as it has a tendency to become quite dark during cooking. Wipe out the pan before melting more butter.)

Serve the French toast with a Preserved Apricot set beside it on each plate, or drizzle the toast with honey, if desired.

Preserved Apricots

MAKES ABOUT 2 CUPS

1 pound fresh, firm, but ripe apricots

2 cups sugar

Begin preparing the preserved apricots about 8 hours before serving. Using a sharp paring knife, cut the apricots in half lengthwise and remove the pits. Arrange the apricot halves, cut-sides up, in a medium (about 3-quart), heavy-bottomed saucepan. Sprinkle the sugar overtop, making sure the apricots are pretty much buried under the sugar. Cover the pan with plastic wrap and set aside at room temperature for at least 8 hours or overnight.

Remove the plastic wrap and set the pan over low heat to begin melting the sugar. (Watch carefully as the sugar melts, reducing the heat or moving the pan on the burner, as necessary, to prevent the sugar from caramelizing or burning.) Simmer the apricots in the sugar syrup, turning them once or twice and skimming any foam that accumulates on the surface, until they are tender and translucent, about 20 minutes. Carefully remove the apricot halves to a sterilized jar (at least 2-cup capacity). Bring the syrup to a boil and cook until the bubbles are big and clear and the syrup is thick, 3 to 5 minutes. Strain the syrup into a small, heatproof bowl and cool to lukewarm.

Pour the cooled syrup over the apricots and seal the jar. Store the apricots in the refrigerator for up to 1 month.

These gorgeous golden scones, speckled with dried cranberries and glistening with sugar, come together so easily and quickly that you could prepare a batch for breakfast while waiting for the coffee to brew. Tender and flaky like old-fashioned scones should be, this version acquires a satisfying nuttiness from the oat bran and a comforting, mild gingerbread quality from the spices and molasses. Crystallized ginger, orange zest, and sweet-tart cranberries contribute a bit of heat, freshness, depth of flavor, and texture.

Gingerbread-Cranberry Scones

MAKES 8 SCONES

1½ cups all-purpose flour
¼ cup oat bran
2 tablespoons packed dark brown sugar
2½ teaspoons baking powder
¾ teaspoon salt
1½ teaspoons ground cinnamon
1 teaspoon ground ginger
½ teaspoon ground cloves
¼ teaspoon freshly grated nutmeg
5 tablespoons cold unsalted butter, cut into cubes, plus more for serving (optional)

2 tablespoons finely chopped crystallized ginger
1 teaspoon grated orange zest
⅓ cup dried cranberries, roughly chopped
2 large eggs
¼ cup cold heavy (whipping) cream, plus more as needed and for brushing
1 tablespoon molasses
Turbinado sugar or other raw or coarse-textured sugar for sprinkling

Apple Butter (page 17) or jam for serving (optional)

Position a rack in the middle of the oven and preheat the oven to 425°F. Line a large baking sheet with parchment paper.

Whisk together the flour, oat bran, brown sugar, baking powder, salt, cinnamon, ginger, cloves, and nutmeg in a large bowl. Add the 5 tablespoons butter and, using a pastry cutter or two knives, cut it into the flour mixture until the pieces are no bigger than the size of small peas. Using a fork, incorporate the crystallized ginger, orange zest, and cranberries. Whisk together the eggs, ¼ cup cream, and molasses in a small bowl. Pour the egg mixture into the flour mixture, mixing lightly with the fork until the dough starts to come together. If the dough seems too dry, drizzle in a little cream at a time until clumps of dough start to form.

Turn the loose bits of dough out onto a lightly floured work surface and knead gently just until the dough comes together. (Overzealous kneading will make for tough scones.) Roll the

dough into a 7-by-7-by-¾-inch square. (This isn't an exact measurement, just a rough estimate.) Using a sharp paring knife, cut the dough into 8 triangles.

Arrange the scones about 2 inches apart on the prepared baking sheet, brush with cream, and sprinkle with turbinado sugar. Bake for about 15 minutes, or until puffed and golden brown.

Cool the scones on the baking sheets set on wire racks for about 1 minute before removing them to the racks to cool further, if desired.

Serve the scones warm or at room temperature with butter, Apple Butter, or jam, if desired. Store the cooled scones in an airtight container or in a zip-top bag for up to 3 days. To warm the scones, arrange them on a parchment-lined baking sheet and heat in a 300°F oven for about 5 minutes.

As with many varieties of decorative gingerbread, we most likely have early German bakers to thank for the gingerbread house. *Lebküchner* (spice-cake bakers) were active in Nuremberg beginning in the late fourteenth century. By the mid-seventeenth century, master bakers joined with candlemakers to form a gingerbread guild. To be sure, these bakers earned prestige in their communities, and their flavorful, often fancifully molded, gingerbreads achieved great notoriety. It seems only natural that this baking tradition eventually gave rise to the popularity of whimsical, edible houses, which gained favor throughout Germany and eventually in America, as well.

CHAPTER SIX: Gingerbread Houses

You need not be a professional pastry chef to create a successful gingerbread house. I have found that with sound templates and some basic instruction, the process is actually fun and gratifying. I have designed two houses for you to try. The first house, a church, actually, is a little more challenging. Creating a wood-frame design with icing, building a steeple, and making "stained-glass" windows out of candy aren't difficult, but they do require a bit more time and patience. The second is a whimsical replica of the circa 1740 Betsy Ross House in Philadelphia. It might appear challenging, but the pieces are really quite basic, and putting them together just takes a bit of time. The brickwork makes this house extra special, but if you don't want to bother with it, just keep it simple and focus on the shingles and other details like the chimney and dormer. With a little practice, you might feel inspired to create your own templates and design your own edible architecture. Think of these as culinary craft projects and have fun with them year-round. Why wait for Christmas?

Working with gingerbread house dough can be challenging. It needs to be fairly firm and dry so that when it bakes, it maintains the shape of your template without puffing or spreading too much. Misshapen house pieces, after all, are a gingerbread architect's worst nightmare. This dough, however, is exceptionally moist and easy to use. It rolls without crumbling, cuts smoothly into shapes, and stays true to the template form in the oven. In addition, unlike some gingerbread house dough, this recipe is really tasty and thus great for making cutout cookies. It stores and freezes well, too, so you can keep it on hand for whenever you feel like building.

Gingerbread House Dough

MAKES ABOUT 4 POUNDS

6 cups all-purpose flour
1¼ teaspoons baking soda
1 teaspoon salt
2½ teaspoons ground ginger
2 teaspoons ground cinnamon
¾ teaspoon ground cloves
½ teaspoon freshly grated nutmeg
1 cup (2 sticks) unsalted butter at room temperature
1¼ cups packed dark brown sugar
¾ cup molasses
½ cup brewed espresso or strong coffee at room temperature
¼ cup water

Whisk together the flour, baking soda, salt, ginger, cinnamon, cloves, and nutmeg in a medium bowl.

Put the butter in the bowl of an electric mixer fitted with the paddle attachment and beat on medium-high speed until smooth. Add the brown sugar and continue beating until light and fluffy. Pour in the molasses and continue mixing until fully incorporated, stopping at least once to scrape the sides of the bowl. Stir together the coffee and water in a small bowl. Reduce the mixing speed to low and alternately add the flour mixture and coffee mixture, beginning and ending with the flour mixture and mixing until just incorporated. Divide the dough in half, placing each half on a large sheet of plastic wrap and shaping them into discs. Wrap tightly and set in the refrigerator to chill for at least 1 hour or overnight.

Position a rack in the middle of the oven and preheat the oven to 350°F. Line baking sheets with parchment paper.

Working with as much dough as necessary to cut your template shapes, roll the dough on a lightly floured work surface to about 3/16 inch thick. Cut the shapes, set on the prepared baking sheets, and bake until firm and golden brown, about 15 minutes. (If your shapes are quite small, you might want to check them at 10 to 12 minutes, removing them once they are firm and golden.)

Set the gingerbread on wire racks to cool completely on the pans. Use the pieces immediately, or arrange them on baking sheets, separated by sheets of parchment or waxed paper; wrap the baking sheets in plastic wrap; and store in a cool, dry area for up to 1 week.

8 pounds (2 recipes) Gingerbread House Dough
(facing page)

Two 7½- to 8-ounce bags multicolored hard candies
Lemon juice, egg whites, or water for thinning the icing

6 cups (about 2 recipes) Royal Icing (page 136)

Green food coloring for the roof
Red food coloring for the door
Yellow food coloring for the door details
White or colored coarse, sanding, or decorating sugar
for the front path (optional)

Roll, cut, and bake the church pieces as directed in the Gingerbread House Dough recipe, using the provided templates. (If you wish, you can make the task a bit easier and omit the back portion of the church. This, of course, will depend on your display area. The template provides an opening for lighting the church using a flashlight or small candle, but without the back wall, the church is easier to illuminate.)

To make the windows, preheat the oven to 300°F and line two large baking sheets with parchment paper. Put the candies in a large zip-top bag and pound with the bottom of a heavy-bottomed pan or rolling pin until the pieces are about the size of lentils. (Some bigger bits are okay, too.) Sprinkle the candy evenly onto the baking sheets in the shape of 11 rectangles (9 large and 2 small), a little bigger than the gingerbread window openings. Put them in the oven to melt for 2 to 5 minutes, or until the candy has completely melted. Set the candy on wire racks to cool completely on the baking sheets. (You can store the windows at this point, covered with plastic wrap and in a cool and dry area, for about 4 days.)

To decorate the walls of the church, add a drizzle of lemon juice (if necessary) to about 1 cup of the royal icing (to start) until it is about the consistency of thick sour cream. The icing needs to be thin enough to pipe, but it shouldn't be runny. Spoon or pour it into a pastry bag fitted with a small round tip (a Number 4 tip is fine here). Pipe the icing in horizontal lines (to simulate wood siding) onto the front, sides, and back pieces. Pipe white dots or beading decoration around the window openings, if desired. Set aside until firm and dry, about 2 hours.

To decorate the roof and steeple, add a drizzle of lemon juice (if necessary) to about 1½ cups of the royal icing (to start) until it is about the consistency of thick sour cream. The icing needs to be thin enough to pipe, but it shouldn't be runny. Tint the icing with green food coloring and spoon or pour the icing into a pastry bag fitted with a small round tip (a Number 4 tip is fine here). Pipe the icing around the edges of the roof and steeple pieces and set aside to dry. Pipe additional horizontal and diagonal lines onto the roof pieces to create a diamond pattern. Spoon some additional icing into a piping bag fitted with a small rosette tip (a Number 24 tip is fine here) and pipe rosettes at the intersections of the lines. Spoon about ½ cup more icing onto the steeple pieces, spreading it evenly to the edges, and set aside until firm and dry, about 2 hours. Add decorative details with thicker royal icing, if desired.

To decorate the door, add enough lemon juice to about ¼ cup of the white icing until it is the consistency of thick heavy (whipping) cream and tint it with a few drops of red food coloring. Pipe the icing onto the facade of the church to create the door and set aside to dry for about 15 minutes. Color about 1 tablespoon of white icing with yellow food coloring and pipe icing hinges, door knobs, and so forth on top of the door, if desired.

To assemble the windows, pipe a bit of thick royal icing around the edges of the windows on the rough sides (undersides) of the church walls. Set the candy windows in place and set aside to dry, about 30 minutes.

To assemble the church, enlist a friend who can help you hold the pieces in place as they dry. Choose a large serving

CONTINUED

platter or board on which you can assemble and display the church. Starting with a front or back piece and one of the sides, pipe thick royal icing onto the edge of one piece and set the other against it at a right angle. Assemble the other sides in the same way (one of you holding the pieces in place while the other pipes icing and moves pieces around). After about 10 minutes, the icing should begin to harden and you can let the pieces dry on their own. If the icing gets a little messy at the corners, wipe it off while it's still wet and decorate the corners with more royal icing later.

To assemble the roof and steeple, use the same techniques as above, holding the pieces in place until they dry.

To finish the church, set it in place on a display table and sprinkle coarse sugar in a path formation leading from the door, if desired. Place a small flashlight or candle at the back of the church to light it (the windows look spectacular this way), if desired.

PHOTOCOPY TEMPLATES AT 300%

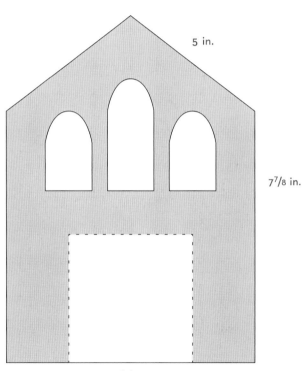

5 in.

7⁷/₈ in.

8 in.

FRONT & BACK (without door)
make one of each

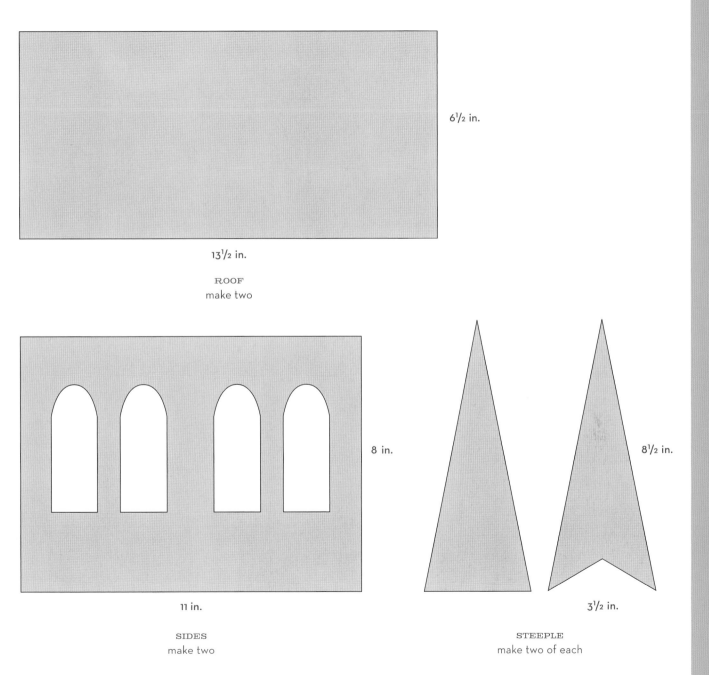

6$\frac{1}{2}$ in.

13$\frac{1}{2}$ in.

ROOF
make two

8 in.

11 in.

SIDES
make two

8$\frac{1}{2}$ in.

3$\frac{1}{2}$ in.

STEEPLE
make two of each

6 pounds (1½ recipes) Gingerbread House Dough (page 122)

Two 7½- to 8-ounce bags butterscotch- or pineapple-flavored (light-colored) hard candies

Lemon juice, egg whites, or water for thinning the icing

6 cups (about 2 recipes) Royal Icing (page 136)

Yellow food coloring for the shutters, door, and roof (optional)

2 tablespoons vodka or water

Red food coloring for the flag

Blue food coloring for the flag

One 3-by-4-inch piece thinly rolled fondant, plus more for the flag stand

One 3- to 4-inch thin pretzel stick

White or colored coarse, sanding, or decorating sugar for the front path (optional)

Roll, cut, and bake the house pieces as directed in the Gingerbread House Dough recipe, using the provided templates. (If you wish, you can make the task a bit easier and omit the back portion of the house. This, of course, will depend on your display area. The template provides an opening for lighting the house using a flashlight or small candle, but without the back wall, the house is easier to illuminate.)

To make the windows, preheat the oven to 300°F and line two large baking sheets with parchment paper. Put the candies in a large zip-top bag and pound with the bottom of a heavy-bottomed pan or rolling pin until the pieces are about the size of lentils. (Some bigger bits are okay, too.) Sprinkle the candy evenly onto the baking sheets in the shape of 12 rough squares, a little bigger than the gingerbread window openings. Put them in the oven to melt for 2 to 5 minutes, or until the candy pieces have completely melted. Set the candy on wire racks to cool on the baking sheets. (You can store the windows at this point, covered with plastic wrap and in a cool and dry area, for about 4 days.)

To decorate the sides of the house and the chimney, add a drizzle of lemon juice to about 1 cup of the royal icing (to start) until it is about the consistency of thick sour cream. The icing needs to be thin enough to pipe, but it shouldn't be runny. Spoon or pour the icing into a pastry bag fitted with a small round tip (a Number 4 tip is fine here). Decorate the sides of the house to create a brickwork pattern, if desired. Pipe the brickwork

pattern onto the chimney pieces. Color some of the icing with yellow food coloring (if desired) and pipe or spread shutters onto the facade. Use white icing to create shutter details and lintels.

To decorate the door, using the same consistency yellow icing you used for the shutters, pipe or spread a rectangular door on the lower right front of the house. Use white icing to create woodwork designs on it as well as a lintel, if desired.

To decorate the roof, add a drizzle of lemon juice (if necessary) to about 1½ cups of the royal icing (to start) until it is about the consistency of cream cheese. Tint the icing with yellow food coloring (if desired) and frost the roof pieces, using a dinner knife or small palette knife.

To decorate the windows, using the same consistency icing you used for the brickwork, pipe windowpane designs onto the melted candy squares.

To assemble the windows, pipe a bit of thick royal icing around the edges of the windows on the rough sides (undersides) of the house walls. Set the candy windows in place and set aside to dry, about 30 minutes.

To assemble the house, enlist a friend who can help you hold the pieces in place as they dry. Choose a large serving platter or board on which you can assemble and display the house. Starting with a front or back piece and one of the sides, pipe thick

CONTINUED

royal icing onto the edge of one piece and set the other against it at a right angle. Assemble the other sides in the same way (one of you holding the pieces in place while the other pipes icing and moves pieces around). After about 10 minutes, the icing should begin to harden and you can let the pieces dry on their own. If the icing gets a little messy at the corners, wipe it off while it's still wet and decorate the corners with more royal icing later.

To assemble the roof, overhang, chimney, and dormer window, use the same techniques as above, holding the pieces in place until they dry. Paste the dormer window in place once the dormer is assembled and glued onto the roof. Pipe icing around the edges of the window to hide the seams.

To make the flag, put about 1 tablespoon of vodka into 2 small bowls and add several drops of red and blue food coloring to each one. Using a small paintbrush, decorate the thinly rolled fondant with the food coloring mixtures and set aside to dry. Paste the flag, using thick royal icing, onto the pretzel stick and set aside to dry. Using an additional golf ball–size round of fondant, shape the fondant into a mound, stand the flag in it, and set it aside until it is fairly firm and stable, about 30 minutes.

To finish the house, set it in place on a display table and sprinkle coarse sugar in a path formation leading from the door, if desired. Place a small flashlight or candle at the back of the house to light it (the windows look spectacular this way), if desired.

PHOTOCOPY TEMPLATES AT 300%

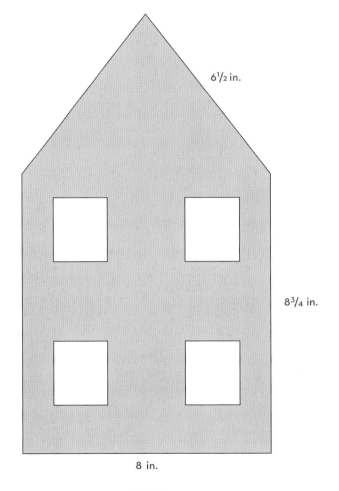

6½ in.

8¾ in.

8 in.

SIDES
make two

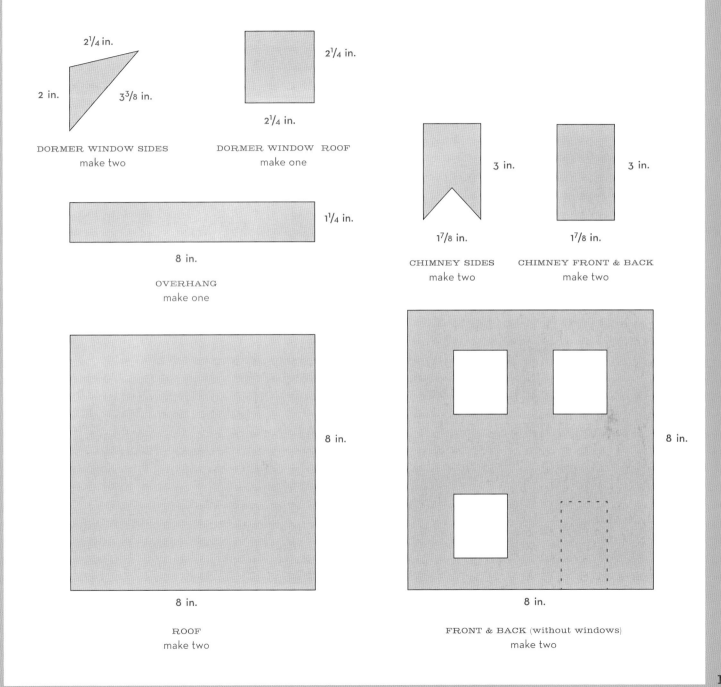

2¼ in.

2 in.   3⅜ in.

DORMER WINDOW SIDES
make two

2¼ in.

2¼ in.

DORMER WINDOW ROOF
make one

1¼ in.

8 in.

OVERHANG
make one

3 in.

3 in.

1⅞ in.   1⅞ in.

CHIMNEY SIDES
make two

CHIMNEY FRONT & BACK
make two

8 in.

8 in.

ROOF
make two

8 in.

8 in.

FRONT & BACK (without windows)
make two

CHAPTER SEVEN: Basics & Accompaniments

Few of the cakes, cookies, and desserts in this book require much in the way of fancy accoutrements. Sometimes, however, a bit of whipped cream, custard sauce, or ice cream adds a nice touch and helps to dress up an otherwise simple gingerbread treat. You will find such recipes in this chapter, as well as some other yummy basics that appear here and there throughout the book. Easy to prepare and useful for keeping on hand, they will add flavor and flair to your gingerbread creations.

Almost every dessert can be made even better with a fluffy mound of whipped cream. It's so basic that you probably don't even need a recipe. I offer one, though, as well as some suggestions, in the hopes of making this easy task even easier. First, whatever amount of cream you use, plan on it just about doubling once it's whipped. Next, and most important in my opinion, stop the whipping process while the cream is still soft. You want light, billowy dollops, not overwhipped, tight spoonfuls. As for the addition of sugar and flavorings, sweeten the cream to your taste and add vanilla extract if you choose. Finally, whipped cream is best when used right away, but you can keep it in the refrigerator for a couple of days if necessary. You never know when dessert emergencies might hit.

→ Whipped Cream ←

MAKES ABOUT 4 CUPS

2 cups heavy (whipping) cream
1 teaspoon vanilla extract (optional)

¼ cup granulated or confectioners' sugar

Pour the cream into the bowl of an electric mixer fitted with the whisk attachment and begin whipping on medium-high speed. Incorporate the vanilla extract (if desired), gradually add the sugar, and continue whipping to soft peaks. Use the cream immediately, or store in an airtight container in the refrigerator for up to 3 days.

One of the first recipes pastry students learn to make is crème anglaise. French for "English cream," this vanilla-scented, egg-rich custard is a delicious all-purpose sauce that closely resembles the custards used for crème brûlée and ice cream. Pastry chefs can make this sauce with their eyes closed, and, with a little practice, you can, too. There are just a few key things to keep in mind. First, take your time tempering the egg yolk and sugar mixture with the hot cream to prevent the eggs from curdling. Next, cook the custard slowly over low heat until it is thick enough to coat the back of a wooden spoon. (Pastry chefs call this stage *nappé*.) When the anglaise is ready, a strainer and large bowl of ice water are your best friends. Have both at the ready to remove any lumpy bits and instantly begin cooling down the hot custard. Know that even experienced pastry chefs occasionally ruin crème anglaise, cooking it for just seconds too long and thus causing it to curdle. You will get the hang of the process, though, in no time. With this crème anglaise recipe in your repertoire, you'll be able to add professional flair to modest and elegant desserts alike.

Crème Anglaise

MAKES 2 CUPS

$1^3/_4$ cups heavy (whipping) cream
1 vanilla bean, or $1^1/_2$ teaspoons vanilla extract
5 large egg yolks

$^1/_3$ cup sugar
$^1/_4$ teaspoon salt

Pour the cream into a medium saucepan. Using a paring knife, split the vanilla bean lengthwise. Scrape out the seeds, using the back of the knife, and put them, along with the bean, into the cream. Slowly bring to a boil over medium-high heat. (If you are using the vanilla extract, wait to add it later.)

Meanwhile, whisk together the egg yolks, sugar, and salt in a large bowl until smooth.

As soon as the cream comes to a boil, gradually drizzle it into the egg yolk mixture while whisking constantly. (Adding the hot cream too quickly will cause the egg yolks to curdle.) Pour the mixture back into the pan and cook over low heat, stirring constantly with a wooden spoon, until it thickens and coats the back of the spoon. (Watch carefully here, as it curdles very quickly after reaching the right thickness. Better to remove it from the heat too early than too late.) Strain the custard into a medium bowl and return the vanilla bean to it. Set the bowl of custard in a larger bowl of ice water to cool, stirring occasionally.

(If using the vanilla extract, add it now.) Cover the custard with plastic wrap and set in the refrigerator to chill completely before using, at least 2 hours. Remove the vanilla bean before serving. Store the crème anglaise in an airtight container in the refrigerator for up to 4 days.

What more is there to say about vanilla ice cream than that it is a delicious, staple treat and makes most desserts that much better? This is a very easy, no-frills recipe, rich with egg yolks, but not overly decadent due to the combination of milk and cream. The focus here is on creating a velvety, vanilla-perfumed base custard. Use a vanilla bean if you can; otherwise, just buy good-quality vanilla extract. Either way, you are sure to be satisfied. This ice cream stores well, too, so you might never have to buy those supermarket cartons again.

⇥ Vanilla Ice Cream ⇤

MAKES ABOUT 1¼ QUARTS

2 cups heavy (whipping) cream
1 cup whole milk
1 vanilla bean, or 2 teaspoons vanilla extract

6 large egg yolks
³⁄₄ cup sugar
¹⁄₄ teaspoon salt

Stir together the cream and milk in a medium (at least 2-quart) saucepan. Using a paring knife, split the vanilla bean lengthwise. Scrape out the seeds, using the back of the knife, and put them, along with the bean, into the cream and milk. Slowly bring to a boil over medium-high heat. (If you are using the vanilla extract, wait to add it later.)

Meanwhile, whisk together the egg yolks, sugar, and salt in a large bowl until thick, smooth, and lemon colored. (Alternatively, you can whip this mixture together using a handheld mixer or a stand mixer fitted with a whisk attachment.)

As soon as the cream mixture comes to a boil, gradually drizzle it into the egg yolk mixture while whisking constantly. (Adding the hot cream too quickly will cause the egg yolks to curdle.) Pour the mixture back into the pan and cook over low heat, stirring constantly with a wooden spoon, until it thickens and coats the back of the spoon. (Watch carefully here, as it curdles very quickly after reaching the right thickness. Better to remove it from the heat too early than too late.) Strain the custard into a medium bowl and return the vanilla bean to it. Set the bowl of custard in a larger bowl of ice water and set aside to cool, stirring occasionally, for about 20 minutes. Cover the custard with plastic wrap and set in the refrigerator to chill completely, at least 4 hours or overnight.

Remove the vanilla bean (or add the vanilla extract now). Pour the mixture into an ice cream machine and process according to the manufacturer's directions.

Spoon the ice cream into a freezer-safe, airtight container and freeze until firm, at least 1 hour before serving. (Store in the container for up to 2 weeks.)

Whenever I prepare to make a wedding cake, one of the first books I turn to is Dede Wilson's *The Wedding Cake Book*. In fact, many of her recipes have inspired not only my wedding cakes, but also fun and fancy cakes I make for a variety of occasions. In my opinion, one of the best recipes in her book is Italian Meringue Buttercream. Most pastry chefs agree that this type of buttercream is superb for filling and covering cakes. Prepared with cooked sugar syrup, Italian buttercream is supremely smooth, glossy, and spreads easily, making frosting and decorating a breeze. It is also deliciously rich and buttery, and not too sweet. I agree with Dede that this buttercream requires a bit more time and attention than other types of buttercreams and frostings, but it is well worth it. I always keep some on hand in case I am called to prepare a cake in a pinch, or, even more important, for when a late-night snack requires a bit of silky buttercream flair.

→ Dede's Italian Buttercream ←

MAKES ABOUT 7 CUPS

½ cup water
1¼ cups plus 5 tablespoons sugar
8 large egg whites (about 1 cup)

1 teaspoon cream of tartar
3 cups (6 sticks) unsalted butter at room temperature

Stir together the water and the 1¼ cups sugar in a small (about 1-quart) saucepan. Bring to a boil, place a candy thermometer in the sugar, and cook to 248°F (firm-ball stage), about 15 minutes. Do not stir the sugar syrup after it has come to a boil, as this will potentially cause it to crystallize. If you notice small crystals forming around the edges of the pan, wash the sides of the pan occasionally with a clean pastry brush dipped in cold water.

Meanwhile, put the egg whites in the bowl of an electric mixer fitted with the whisk attachment and whip on medium-high speed until frothy. Add the cream of tartar, gradually sprinkle in the remaining 5 tablespoons of sugar, and continue to whip to soft peaks. (Ideally, you want the meringue and sugar syrup to be ready at the same time. If the meringue is close to being ready, reduce the mixing speed to low while waiting for the sugar syrup. Increase the speed again to finish the meringue once the sugar syrup is ready.)

As soon as the sugar syrup reaches the desired temperature, remove the saucepan from the heat and reduce the meringue mixing speed to medium-low. Gradually incorporate the sugar syrup into the whipping meringue, allowing it to drizzle in a thin, steady stream down the side of the bowl. (This will prevent the sugar from forming hard strands around the interior of the bowl.) As soon as all of the sugar syrup is incorporated, increase the mixing speed to high and whip the meringue until it is thick and the bowl is cool to the touch.

Reduce the mixing speed to medium-high and gradually incorporate the butter, about 1 tablespoon at a time. Continue whipping until the buttercream is smooth, glossy, and light. Use the buttercream immediately, or store it in an airtight container for up to 1 week in the refrigerator or up to 2 months in the freezer. To use it from the chilled state, bring the firm buttercream to room temperature, or heat it gradually in the microwave at about 10-second intervals until slightly softened. This will prevent the buttercream from breaking when it is whipped.

NOTE
If the buttercream breaks after you have incorporated the butter, the butter might have been too cold. Don't worry. Simply warm the bowl (as the buttercream is whipping) with your hands, place a warm, damp towel around it, or rub it with a warm, damp sponge.

Versatile and easy to prepare, royal icing is indispensable for decorating cookies and cakes, as well as building, and adding flair to, gingerbread houses. The consistency depends on how much liquid (in this case egg whites) you incorporate into the confectioners' sugar. The following recipe will do nicely for constructing gingerbread houses, as it's quite thick. For decorating the houses as well as cutout cookies, a bit more egg white will enable you to create detailed designs. Add even more egg whites, and you'll have thin (flow or flooding) icing that you can spread easily over larger areas. In addition to egg whites, I also like to thin my icing with lemon juice. It not only adds a bright, fresh flavor, but it also turns the icing sparkling white. This recipe calls for fresh egg whites, but you can also use the pasteurized variety. I like the pasteurized organic egg whites sold in the refrigerated organic section of most supermarkets. If you choose this option, count on about 2 to 3 tablespoons of pasteurized whites for each large, fresh egg white. Royal icing (especially when thick) becomes hard very quickly. Take as much as you need and then cover the remainder with plastic wrap, setting the wrap directly on top of the icing to prevent it from drying. Stored this way, at room temperature or in the refrigerator, it will keep fresh and soft for a couple of days.

Royal Icing

MAKES ABOUT 3 CUPS

4 cups (1 pound) confectioners' sugar

1/2 teaspoon cream of tartar

4 large fresh or pasteurized egg whites

Combine the confectioners' sugar and cream of tartar in the bowl of an electric mixer fitted with the paddle attachment and begin beating on medium-low speed. Add the egg whites, increase the mixing speed to high, and continue beating until the icing is smooth, thick, and glossy, about 7 minutes, stopping at least once to scrape the sides and bottom of the bowl. (If you're working on a particularly dry day, you might need to drizzle in more egg whites to reach this consistency.)

Scrape the icing into a bowl and cover with plastic wrap, placing the wrap directly on top of the icing to prevent it from drying. (Use the icing immediately, or store it in an airtight container in the refrigerator for up to 2 days. Warm the icing to room temperature before beating again until smooth.)

NOTE

To make royal icing suitable for spreading on cookies (flow or flooding icing), spoon some of the thick icing into a bowl. Drizzle in a bit of egg white or lemon juice, just a few drops at a time, stirring until the icing reaches the desired consistency.

Whether you're coating cookies or truffles, or just need a drizzle of chocolate decoration, this glaze will do the trick nicely. It is easy to prepare and dries to a hard, smooth finish. Once it becomes firm, the glaze stores well for several weeks. Simply melt it again in a bowl over simmering water or in the microwave when you need a bit of chocolate panache.

→ Dark Chocolate Glaze ←

MAKES 1½ CUPS

12 ounces bittersweet chocolate, chopped

¼ cup vegetable oil

Put the chocolate in a medium, heatproof bowl. Set the bowl over a saucepan filled with about 1½ inches of simmering water (being sure not to let the bottom of the bowl touch the water) and stir occasionally until the chocolate is melted and smooth. (You can also melt the chocolate in the microwave, heating it at about 20-second intervals and stirring periodically until it is melted and smooth.) Remove the bowl from the saucepan and stir in the vegetable oil.

Use the glaze immediately to drizzle or coat. If you are using the glaze later, pour it into an airtight container, set aside until firm, and store in a cool area or in the refrigerator for up to 1 month.

NOTE

To melt the glaze once it becomes hard, repeat the procedure for melting the chocolate.

Every time I purchase candied orange peel I wonder why I didn't make it myself. The store-bought variety is usually expensive, and it never tastes really fresh. This recipe will save you the same remorse. It requires a bit of time at the stove, and the peel takes a while to dry, but your efforts will be rewarded in the end. Homemade candied orange peel is full of flavor and keeps well for weeks. The same process works with lemon peel, too. You'll never buy the supermarket stuff again.

Candied Orange Peel

MAKES ABOUT 11¼ OUNCES

4 large navel oranges
3 cups sugar

1½ cups water
¼ cup light corn syrup

Using a sharp chef's knife or paring knife, trim the ends of the oranges. Sit each orange upright on a flat work surface. Using the paring knife and following the contour of the orange, cut the peel away in strips from the fruit. The strips don't have to be of any particular width, and it's okay if they have some pith (white part) on them, too.

Put the orange strips in a medium saucepan, pour in cold water just to cover them, and bring to a boil over medium-high heat. As soon as the water begins to boil, drain the peel immediately. Repeat the process two more times. (This technique softens the peel and reduces its bitterness.)

Using the same pan, combine 2 cups of the sugar, the water, and corn syrup. Bring to a simmer over medium heat, stirring occasionally to dissolve the sugars.

Meanwhile, trim the blanched peel of any white pith and slice the pieces lengthwise into thin strips, about ¼ inch thick.

Carefully drop the peel into the simmering sugar syrup. Reduce the heat to low and cook at a very slow simmer until the peel is tender and translucent, about 1 hour.

Remove the pan from the heat and set aside to cool completely. Cover the pan with plastic wrap and set aside for at least 8 hours or overnight.

Carefully drain the orange peel, reserving the syrup, if desired. (The syrup has a lovely orange aroma and flavor. Use it for sweetening beverages, or use it to candy another batch of orange peel.) Arrange the strips on a wire rack (the pieces should not touch) and set aside in a cool area to dry for at least 8 hours or overnight. The peel will still be slightly sticky to the touch when it's ready.

Put the remaining 1 cup of the sugar in a shallow pan or bowl. Toss the dried peel a small handful at a time in the sugar to generously coat. Arrange the peel again on a wire rack and set aside in a cool area to dry for at least 8 hours or overnight. The candied peel will be firm and crystallized when it's ready. (Use the peel immediately, or store it in an airtight container in a cool, dry area for up to 2 months.)

NOTE
To prepare candied lemon peel, use 6 lemons and proceed with the recipe in the same manner.

Acknowledgments

All writing is a solitary business. Even writing about food requires many hours alone at the computer. Sure, there are the busy afternoons in the kitchen when music and talk radio make for welcome companions, but they ask little of us. Happily, while others play sonatas or talk about politics, we cook-writers are disconnected enough to focus on the tasks at hand, free to drown out ambient noise with the mixer. Yes, at the end of the day and with a house perfumed from cooking endeavors, even food writers must struggle with finding the right words, turns of phrase, and stories that make up the (hopefully perfect) literary baby we finally deliver to our editors in manuscript form.

*

The thing of it is, however, once the offspring lands in the waiting arms of the publisher, the solitary act of writing and creating dissipates with astonishing speed like a drop of water on a hot griddle. Editors, art directors, and designers shape and nurture the text, coddling and coaxing it into a mature and beautiful work. We writers like to think our books are ours and ours alone, but, really, they are the result of many talented folks whose skills breathe life into them—hopefully for a long time.

I am grateful for having worked with such a gifted team at Chronicle Books who, through terrific editing, design, and direction, imbued *Gingerbread* with such tempting spirit. Thank you, first, to Bill LeBlond, who gave me the opportunity to write this book and is always so generous with his support. Thanks, too, to Anne Donnard, my art director and designer, who gave the words on the page shape and clarity through creative images and an eye-catching layout. Thank you to Amy Treadwell and Sarah Billingsley, my editors, who critiqued the text and caringly kneaded it into its present form, and to Doug Ogan, my managing editor, who attended to many of the vital and most important final details.

Thank you, as well, Béatrice Peltre, my photographer, for your gifted eye, fresh vision, and creative spirit. Your artistic images give just the right expression to the recipes. It was great fun cooking and working with you. I am grateful for your hard work and am even more honored by your friendship.

Thank you, Liv and Bill Blumer, my agent team, for working so diligently on the business details so I could focus on cooking and writing. I am grateful for your clarity, support, and for your consistently thoughtful advice.

There are those, too, who encouraged this project for years before it ever reached proposal stage and who were always ready with kind nudges during the solitary days of writing and recipe testing. Thank you, Antonia Allegra, Don and Joan Fry, and Diane Morgan for tirelessly believing in my ideas and abilities and for all of your thoughtful advice. Thank you, Dorie Greenspan, for offering me such kind, encouraging, and calming words as I neared my deadline. Thank you, too, Anne Willan, for inspiring me with your own beautiful books and for giving me the opportunity to form many of my ideas about this project at your enchanting Château du Feÿ.

Thank you, as well, to all of my friends and family who tasted countless recipes over the months without complaint and offered such helpful feedback. Thank you, Grandmom Lindner, for inspiring me to love cooking and appreciate good food at an early age, and for sharing yourself with me through your recipes. To my parents, Albert and Carol Lee Lindner, I can't express enough how much I (once again) appreciate your gracious and undying support (as well as the occasional use of your kitchen). To my sister Erica, thank you for all of your good ideas and especially for the honest feedback your children always so candidly offer. To my sister Alexis, thank you for so often being such a helpful and fun second pair of hands in the kitchen. Thank you, finally, to my husband, Chris, who continues to give me the freedom to dream, to write, to cook, and to create. (Yes, there is still a container of buttercream in the freezer.)

Table of Equivalents

The exact equivalents in the following tables have been rounded for convenience.

*

U.S.	Metric
¼ teaspoon	1.25 milliliters
½ teaspoon	2.5 milliliters
1 teaspoon	5 milliliters
1 tablespoon (3 teaspoons)	15 milliliters
1 fluid ounce (2 tablespoons)	30 milliliters
¼ cup	60 milliliters
⅓ cup	80 milliliters
½ cup	120 milliliters
1 cup	240 milliliters
1 pint (2 cups)	480 milliliters
1 quart (4 cups, 32 ounces)	960 milliliters
1 gallon (4 quarts)	3.84 liters
1 ounce (by weight)	28 grams
1 pound	454 grams
2.2 pounds	1 kilogram

U.S.	Metric
⅛ inch	3 millimeters
¼ inch	6 millimeters
½ inch	12 millimeters
1 inch	2.5 centimeters

Fahrenheit	Celsius	Gas
250	120	½
275	140	1
300	150	2
325	160	3
350	180	4
375	190	5
400	200	6
425	220	7
450	230	8
475	240	9
500	260	10